# BE
## COMFORTED

# BE

## COMFORTED

### FEELING SECURE IN THE ARMS OF GOD

## OT COMMENTARY

## ISAIAH

# Warren W. Wiersbe

DAVID C COOK

*transforming lives together*

BE COMFORTED
Published by David C Cook
4050 Lee Vance Drive
Colorado Springs, CO 80918 U.S.A.

Integrity Music Limited, a Division of David C Cook
Brighton, East Sussex BN1 2RE, England

The graphic circle C logo is a registered trademark of David C Cook.

Library of Congress Control Number 2009923009
ISBN 978-1-4347-6615-1
eISBN 978-0-7814-0098-5

First edition of *Be Comforted* by Warren W. Wiersbe published by Victor Books®
in 1992 © Warren W. Wiersbe, ISBN 0-89693-797-6

The Team: Karen Lee-Thorp, Amy Kiechlin, Jack Campbell, and Susan Vannaman
Series Cover Design: John Hamilton Design
Cover Photo: Getty Images
Study Questions: Susan Moroney

Printed in the United States of America

Second Edition 2009

13 14 15 16 17 18 19 20 21 22

030320

# CONTENTS

# THE BIG IDEA

## An Introduction to *Be Comforted*
## by Ken Baugh

His name was Sir Ernest Henry Shackleton. His goal was to lead the first expedition across the South Polar continent known as Antarctica. However, before this expedition ended, Shackleton and his crew faced gale force winds over 150 miles per hour, bone-chilling temperatures of 100 degrees below zero, 80-foot seas, hunger, and the oppressively dark days of the Antarctic winter. In his book *Endurance: Shackleton's Incredible Voyage*, Alfred Lansing describes this darkness:

> In all the world there is no desolation more complete than the polar night. It is a return to the ice age—no warmth, no life, no movement. Only those who have experienced it can appreciate what it means to be without the sun day after day and week after week. Few men unaccustomed to it can fight off its effects altogether, and it has driven some men mad. (p. vii)

And yet in spite of these conditions, nothing could prepare Shackleton's crew for the devastating destruction of their vessel, aptly named the *Endurance*.

The *Endurance* became trapped in the icy Weddell Sea and forced the crew to survive through extreme conditions for an entire Antarctic winter. However, once the spring thaw began, instead of being released from its frozen prison, the ship was crushed by large blocks of floating ice. These damaged the hull beyond repair and left the entire expedition stranded.

Mounting all the courage and strength they could muster, the men loaded into the three remaining lifeboats and began rowing toward Elephant Island, 100 miles away. By the time they reached the island, it was the first time in 497 days that they had stood on solid ground. But their ordeal was not over yet. Elephant Island was outside the main shipping channels, and nobody knew they were there, so they had no hope of rescue. Their only chance for survival was to add a makeshift sail to one of the lifeboats and attempt to sail from Elephant Island to the South Georgia Whaling station.

There was only one small problem with this: South Georgia was 800 miles away! Resolved to save his men, Captain Shackleton chose four others and set sail for South Georgia on April 24, promising those he was leaving behind that he would come back for them. Miraculously, on May 9, they sighted South Georgia, but the winds made a landing impossible, so they waited until morning. During the night, a full-blown hurricane hit, and they thought it was the end. But again, by some miracle they survived the night drifting in their lifeboat and landed on the unoccupied southern shore of South Georgia the next morning. Fearing that putting out to sea again to reach the whaling station would be too dangerous, Shackleton made a land crossing by foot that had never been attempted before. It took him and two of the other men thirty-six hours to reach the whaling station at Stromness.

Without delay, he assembled a rescue party to get the men he had left behind on Elephant Island, but his first three attempts failed due to rough seas and bad weather. Finally, he secured a small tugboat from the Chilean Navy and rescued all twenty-two of his stranded men. Shackleton had kept his promise to return. Wow! What an incredible story of courage and devotion. Shackleton loved his men so much that he risked his life numerous times to save them.

The trials surrounding this event in the life of Sir Ernest Shackleton remind me of the Big Idea that runs throughout the book of Isaiah, namely that the Lord saves. According to Isaiah, Jesus is the Savior who is coming, the Savior who came, and the Savior who is coming back one day. Let's take a look at these three dynamics in regard to our God who saves in the book of Isaiah.

First, Isaiah said that a Savior was coming (predicted in Isaiah 7:14; 9:6–7; fulfilled in Matthew 1:18–25). He said this Savior would come through the line of Jesse, the father of King David (predicted in Isaiah 11:1; fulfilled in Luke 3:23, 32). Isaiah recorded these prophecies seven hundred years before Jesus was born. Jesus Christ is the Messiah, our Savior whom Isaiah said would come.

Second, Isaiah said what would happen to the Savior once He came. The Savior would perform miracles (predicted in Isaiah 35:5–6; fulfilled in Matthew 9:35). He would be rejected by His own people (predicted in Isaiah 53:3; fulfilled in John 7:5, 48). He would stand silent before His accusers (predicted in Isaiah 53:7; fulfilled in Matthew 27:12). He would be wounded and bruised (predicted in Isaiah 53:5; fulfilled in Matthew 27:26), smitten and spit upon (predicted in Isaiah 50:6; fulfilled in Matthew 26:67). He would pray for His persecutors (predicted in Isaiah 53:12; fulfilled in Luke 23:34). He would be crucified with two thieves (predicted in Isaiah 53:9; fulfilled in Matthew 27:38). He would be buried in a rich man's tomb (predicted in Isaiah 53:9; fulfilled in Matthew 27:57–60). Again, Jesus was the One who fulfilled all of these prophecies, and He did so to pay the price for my sin and yours, so that through faith in Him, we might gain forgiveness and eternal life. Jesus Christ is the Messiah, our Savior who Isaiah said would come to suffer and die in our place.

Finally, Isaiah said the Savior will come back again one day to set up a literal kingdom on earth and usher in a time of prosperity, peace, and joy (Isa. 2:2–5; 32:1–8; 35). The Bible describes this time as the millennial kingdom when Jesus will personally reign on the earth for a thousand years. Jesus made two incredible promises to His followers. First, He promised that after He rose from the dead, He would go and prepare a place for us in His Father's house. And second, Jesus promised that He would come back for us, to take us to be with Him forever (John 14:1–4). This means that when Jesus comes back to earth, we will reign with Him too (Zech. 14:9; 2 Tim. 2:12). No matter what happens in this life, my friend, nothing can change the fact that our God has saved us and that in Him we have a glorious hope and future. As I have heard Dr. Dallas Willard say, "We are in training for reigning." Take comfort in that!

***

Dr. Wiersbe's commentaries have been a source of guidance and strength to me over the many years that I have been a pastor. His unique style is not overly academic, but theologically sound. He explains the deep truths of Scripture in a way that everyone can understand and apply. Whether you're a Bible scholar or a brand-new believer in Christ, you will benefit, as I have, from Warren's insights. With your Bible in one hand and Dr. Wiersbe's commentary in the other, you will be able to accurately unpack the deep truths of God's Word and learn how to apply them to your life.

Drink deeply, my friend, of the truths of God's Word, for in them you will find Jesus Christ, and there is freedom, peace, assurance, and joy.

—Ken Baugh
Pastor of Coast Hills Community Church
Aliso Viejo, California

# A WORD FROM THE AUTHOR

"Isaiah is great for two reasons," wrote William Sanford LaSor in his fascinating book *Great Personalities of the Old Testament* (Revell, 136): "He lived in momentous days, in critical days of international upheaval, and he wrote what many consider to be the greatest book in the Old Testament."

"We see Isaiah move with fearless dignity through the chaos of his day," wrote E. M. Blaiklock, "firm in his quiet faith, sure in his God" (*Handbook of Bible People*, Scripture Union, 329).

At a time when empires were rising and falling and his nation was in peril, Isaiah wrote, "In returning and rest you shall be saved; in quietness and confidence shall be your strength" (30:15 NKJV). And when a new generation faced the arduous task of rebuilding a ruined nation, it was the words of Isaiah the prophet that gave them courage: "But those who wait on the LORD shall renew their strength; they shall mount up with wings like eagles, they shall run and not be weary, they shall walk and not faint" (40:31 NKJV).

Isaiah is the prophet we need to hear today as he cries out God's message above the din of world upheaval, "Comfort, yes, comfort My people!" (40:1 NKJV). The English word *comfort* comes from two Latin words that together mean "with strength." When Isaiah says to us, "Be comforted!" it is not a word of pity but of power. God's comfort does not weaken us; it strengthens us. God is not indulging us but empowering us. "In quietness and confidence shall be your strength."

As we study Isaiah's book, we shall meet not only this outstanding prophet, but also some mighty kings and rulers; and we shall witness the rise and fall of magnificent kingdoms. We shall see God's people chastened and then restored. But above all else, we shall see the Lord Jesus Christ, God's "Suffering Servant," as He does the will of God and suffers and dies for the sins of the world.

My own faith in God was strengthened as I walked with Isaiah during the months I wrote *Be Comforted*. I trust that your faith will also be strengthened as together we listen to the Word of God through Isaiah the prophet.

—Warren W. Wiersbe

# A SUGGESTED OUTLINE OF THE BOOK OF ISAIAH

Theme: The salvation (deliverance) of the Lord
Key verse: Isaiah 1:18

I.  Condemnation (Isaiah 1—39)
    A.  Sermons Against Judah and Israel (Isaiah 1—12)
    B.  Burdens of Judgment Against the Gentiles (Isaiah 13—23)
    C.  Songs About Future Glory (Isaiah 24—27)
    D.  Woes of Coming Judgment from Assyria (Isaiah 28—35)
    E.  Historical Interlude (Isaiah 36—39)
        1. Hezekiah delivered from Assyria (Isaiah 36—37)
        2. Hezekiah deceived by Babylon (Isaiah 37—38)

II. Consolation (Isaiah 40—66)
    A.  God's Greatness (Isaiah 40—48) (the Father versus idols)
    B.  God's Grace (Isaiah 49—57) (the Son, God's Servant)
    C.  God's Glory (Isaiah 58—66) (the Spirit and the kingdom)

# Chapter One

# THE LORD IS SALVATION

## (Introduction to Isaiah)

Sir Winston Churchill was once asked to give the qualifications a person needed in order to succeed in politics, and he replied: "It is the ability to foretell what is going to happen tomorrow, next week, next month, and next year. And to have the ability afterwards to explain why it didn't happen."

Because God's prophets were correct all of the time, they didn't have to explain away their mistakes. "If what a prophet proclaims in the name of the LORD does not take place or come true," wrote Moses, "that is a message the LORD has not spoken" (Deut. 18:22 NIV). "To the law and to the testimony," wrote Isaiah, "if they speak not according to this word, it is because there is no light in them" (8:20). Isaiah was a man who had God's light, and he was not afraid to let it shine.

Before we examine the text of Isaiah's prophecy, let's get acquainted with the background of the book so that we can better understand the man and his times.

### THE MAN

The name *Isaiah* means "salvation of the Lord," and salvation (deliverance) is the key theme of his book. He wrote concerning five different acts of deliverance

*5 acts of deliverance:*

that God would perform: (1) the deliverance of Judah from Assyrian invasion (chaps. 36—37); (2) the deliverance of the nation from Babylonian captivity (chap. 40); (3) the future deliverance of the Jews from worldwide dispersion among the Gentiles (chaps. 11—12); (4) the deliverance of lost sinners from judgment (chap. 53); and (5) the final deliverance of creation from the bondage of sin when the kingdom is established (chaps. 60; 66:17ff.).

There were other Jewish men named Isaiah, so the prophet identified himself seven times as "the son of Amoz," not to be confused with "Amos" (see 1:1; 2:1; 13:1; 20:2; 37:2, 21; 38:1). Isaiah was married, and his wife was called "the prophetess" (8:3), either because she was married to a prophet or because she shared the prophetic gift. He fathered two sons whose names have prophetic significance: Shearjashub ("a remnant shall return," 7:3) and Maher-shalal-hash-baz ("quick to plunder, swift to the spoil," 8:1–4, 18). The two names speak of the nation's judgment and restoration, two important themes in Isaiah's prophecy.

Isaiah was called to his ministry "in the year that King Uzziah died" (6:1), which was 739 BC. Isaiah ministered through the reigns of Jotham, Ahaz, and Hezekiah, who died in 686. Tradition says that Manasseh, King Hezekiah's successor, killed Isaiah by having him sawn in half (Heb. 11:37), but there is no record of this in Scripture.

What kind of man was Isaiah the prophet? As you read his prophecy, you will discover that he was a man in touch with God. He saw God's Son and God's glory (chap. 6; John 12:41), he heard God's message, and he sought to bring the nation back to God before it was too late.

Isaiah was a man who loved his nation. The phrase "my people" is used at least twenty-six times in his book. He was a patriot with a true love for his country, pleading with Judah to return to God and warning kings when their foreign policy was contrary to God's will. The American political leader Adlai Stevenson called patriotism "not a short and frenzied outburst of emotion, but the tranquil and steady dedication of a life." He was not thinking of Isaiah when he said that, but Stevenson's words perfectly describe the prophet and his work.

He was also a man who hated sin and sham religion. His favorite name for God is "the Holy One of Israel," and he uses it twenty-five times in his book. (It is used only five times in the rest of the Old Testament.) He looked at the crowded courts of the temple and cried out, "They have forsaken the LORD, they have provoked the Holy One of Israel unto anger, they are gone away backward" (1:4). He examined the political policies of the leaders and said, "Woe to them that go down to Egypt for help ... but they look not unto the Holy One of Israel, neither seek the LORD!" (31:1). Jehovah was holy, but the nation was sinful, and Isaiah called the people to repent.

Isaiah was certainly a courageous man. Unafraid to denounce kings and priests, and unwavering when public opinion went against him, he boldly declared the Word of God. For three years Isaiah wore only a loincloth to dramatize the victory of Assyria over Egypt (chap. 20). In so doing, he hoped to get the attention of people who were blind to their country's danger.

He was a man skilled in communicating God's truth. Not content with merely declaring facts, Isaiah clothed those facts in striking language that would catch the attention of a people blind and deaf to spiritual truth (6:9–10). He compared the nation to a diseased body (1:5–6), a harlot (v. 21), a useless vineyard (chap. 5), a bulging wall about to fall down (30:13), and a woman in travail (66:8). Assyria, the enemy, would come like a swollen stream (8:7–8), a swarm of bees (7:18), a lion (5:29), and an axe (10:15). Like our Lord Jesus Christ, Isaiah knew how to stir the imagination of his listeners so that he might arouse their interest and teach them God's truth (Matt. 13:10–17).

## THE MONARCHS

Isaiah prophesied during the days of "Uzziah, Jotham, Ahaz, and Hezekiah, kings of Judah" (1:1). The nation had divided after the death of Solomon (1 Kings 12), but the priesthood and the Davidic throne belonged to

Judah. The ten northern tribes formed the kingdom of Israel (Ephraim), with Samaria as its capital city, and Benjamin and Judah united to form the kingdom of Judah, with Jerusalem as its capital city. Though Isaiah predicted the fall of Israel to Assyria (chap. 28), which occurred in 722 BC, his major focus was on Judah and Jerusalem (1:1).

Uzziah is also called Azariah. At the age of sixteen, he became coregent with his father, Amaziah, and was on the throne for fifty-two years (792–740). When his father was assassinated in 767, Uzziah became the sole ruler and brought the nation to its greatest days since David and Solomon (2 Kings 14:17–22; 15:1–7; 2 Chron. 26:1–15). "But when he was strong, his heart was lifted up to his destruction" (2 Chron. 26:16). He tried to intrude into the priest's ministry in the temple, and God judged him by smiting him with leprosy. It was in the year that King Uzziah died that Isaiah was called to minister (Isa. 6:1).

Jotham was coregent after his father became a leper, and his record as king was a good one (2 Kings 15:32–38; 2 Chron. 27). He reigned for twenty years, and it was during his time that the Assyrian Empire began to emerge as a new and threatening power. During the last twelve years of Jotham's reign, his son Ahaz served as coregent, but Ahaz was not one of Judah's good kings.

Ahaz forged political alliances that eventually brought Judah into bondage to Assyria (2 Kings 16; 2 Chron. 28). Judah was repeatedly threatened by Egypt from the south and by Syria and Israel from the north, and Ahaz depended on an alliance with Assyria to protect himself. Isaiah warned Ahaz that his alliances with godless Gentiles would not work, and he encouraged the king to put his trust in the Lord (Isa. 7).

Hezekiah reigned forty-two years and was one of Judah's greatest kings (2 Kings 18—20; 2 Chron. 29—32). He not only strengthened the city of Jerusalem and the nation of Judah, but led the people back to the Lord. He built the famous water system that still exists in Jerusalem.

The ministry of Isaiah spans a period of over fifty years, from 739 BC (the death of Uzziah) to 686 BC (the death of Hezekiah), and it probably extended into the early years of King Manasseh's reign. It was a difficult time of international upheaval, when first one power and then another threatened Judah. But the greatest dangers were not outside the nation: They were within. In spite of the godly leadership of King Hezekiah, Judah had no more godly kings. One by one, Hezekiah's successors led the nation into political and spiritual decay, ending in captivity in Babylon.

The British expositor G. Campbell Morgan said, "The whole story of the prophet Isaiah, as it is revealed to us in this one book, is that of a man who spoke to an inattentive age or to an age which, if attentive, mocked him and refused to obey his message, until, as the prophetic period drew to a close, he inquired in anguish, 'Who hath believed our report? And to whom hath the arm of the Lord been revealed?'" (*Westminster Pulpit*, vol. 10, p. 10)

## THE MESSAGE

Isaiah opened his book with a series of sermons denouncing sin: the personal sins of the people (chaps. 1—6) and the national sins of the leaders (chaps. 7—12). In these messages, he warned of judgment and pled for repentance. The prophets Amos and Hosea were preaching similar messages to the people of the northern kingdom, warning them that time was running out.

But the Gentile nations around Judah and Israel were not innocent! In chapters 13—23, Isaiah denounced those nations for their sins and warned of God's judgment. Israel and Judah had sinned against the law of God and were even more guilty than their neighbors, but the Gentile nations would not escape God's wrath. In the way they had behaved, these nations had sinned against conscience (Rom. 2:1–16) and against human decency. The prophet Amos was preaching the same message in the northern kingdom, but he denounced the Gentiles first and then warned the Jews (Amos 1—2).

As you study the book of Isaiah, you will discover that the prophet interspersed messages of hope with words of judgment. God remembers His mercy even when declaring His wrath (Hab. 3:2), and He assures His people that they have a "hope and a future" (Jer. 29:11 NIV). Isaiah 24—27 is devoted to "songs of hope" that describe the glory of the future kingdom. Isaiah saw a day when the two kingdoms of Israel and Judah would return to the land, be reunited and redeemed, and enter into the blessings of the promised kingdom.

Chapters 28—35 focus on the impending Assyrian invasion of Israel and Judah. Israel would be destroyed and the ten tribes assimilated into the Assyrian Empire. (This is the origin of the Samaritans, who were part Jewish and part Gentile.) Judah would be invaded and devastated, but Jerusalem would be delivered by the Lord.

At this point in his book, Isaiah moved from prophecy to history and focused on two key events that occurred during the reign of King Hezekiah: God's miraculous deliverance of Jerusalem from the Assyrians (chaps. 36—37), and Hezekiah's foolish cooperation with the Babylonians (chaps. 38—39). This section forms a transition from an emphasis on Assyria to an emphasis on Babylon, for the last twenty-seven chapters look ahead to the return of the Jewish remnant from Babylonian captivity.

The Jewish rabbis call Isaiah 40—66 "The Book of Consolation," and their description is accurate. Addressed originally to the discouraged Jewish exiles returning to an impoverished land and a ruined temple, these chapters have brought comfort and hope to God's people in every age and in every kind of difficult situation. The Hebrew word translated "comfort" also means "to repent." God brings comfort, not to rebellious people but to repentant people.

The arrangement of chapters 40—66 is not accidental. "The Book of Consolation" is divided into three sections; each focuses on a different

Person of the Godhead and a different attribute of God. Chapters 40—48 exalt the greatness of God the Father; chapters 49—57, the grace of God the Son, God's Suffering Servant; and chapters 58—66, the glory of the future kingdom when the Spirit is poured out on God's people. Note the references to the Spirit in 59:19, 21; 61:1; and 63:10–11, 14.

*Servant* is one of the key words in this second section of the book of Isaiah. The word is used seventeen times and has three different referents: the nation of Israel (41:8–9; 43:10); Cyrus, king of Persia, whom God raised up to help Israel restore their nation and rebuild their temple (44:28; 45:1; see Ezra 1:1); and Jesus Christ, the Son of God (Isa. 42:1, 19; 52:13; 53:11), the Suffering Servant who died for the sins of the world. While Assyria and Egypt vie for the center stage in chapters 1—39, it is Babylon and Persia that get the attention in chapters 40—66.

In summary, Isaiah had an immediate word of warning to both Israel and Judah that Assyria was on the march and would be used by God to punish them for their sins. Occasionally, Isaiah used this invasion to picture "the day of the Lord," that future time when the whole world will taste of the wrath of God. The prophets often used immediate circumstances to illustrate future events.

Isaiah had a word of promise to Judah that God would deliver Jerusalem from the enemy for the sake of David's throne. There was also a word of hope for the future Jewish exiles in Babylon, that God would rescue them and help them restore their nation and their temple. But Isaiah's greatest message is his word of salvation, announcing the coming of the Messiah, the Servant of the Lord, who would die for sinners and one day return to earth to establish His glorious kingdom.

## THE MESSIAH

Isaiah was much more than a prophet. He was an evangelist who presented Jesus Christ and the good news of the gospel. Isaiah's "Servant Song" about

Jesus (Isa. 52:13—53:12) is quoted or alluded to nearly forty times in the New Testament.

The prophet wrote about the birth of Christ (Isa. 7:14; 9:6; Matt. 1:18–25); the ministry of John the Baptist (Isa. 40:1–6; Matt. 3:1ff.); Christ's anointing by the Spirit (Isa. 61:1–2; Luke 4:17–19); the nation's rejection of their Messiah (Isa. 6:9–11; John 12:38ff.); Christ, the "stone of stumbling" (Isa. 8:14; 28:16; Rom. 9:32–33; 10:11; 1 Peter 2:6); Christ's ministry to the Gentiles (Isa. 49:6; Luke 2:32; Acts 13:47); the Savior's suffering and death (Isa. 52:13—53:12; Acts 3:13; 8:32–33; 1 Peter 2:21–25); His resurrection (Isa. 55:3; Acts 13:34); and His return to reign as King (Isa. 9:6–7; 11:1ff.; 59:20–21; 63:1–3; Rom. 11:26–27; Rev. 19:13–15). There are many other references in Isaiah to the Messiah, and we will identify them as we study this book.

It is this emphasis on redemption that gives Isaiah a message for the whole world. While it is true he ministered to the little nation of Judah and wrote about nations and empires that for the most part are no longer on the world scene, his focus was on God's plan of salvation for the whole world. Isaiah saw the greatness of God and the vastness of His plan of salvation for Jews and Gentiles alike. Isaiah was a patriot but not a bigot; he saw beyond his own nation to the gracious work God would do among the Gentile nations of the world.

I have a feeling that the book of Isaiah was a favorite book of the apostle Paul. He quoted from it or alluded to it at least eighty times in his Epistles and in at least three of his recorded messages (Acts 13:34, 47; 17:24–29; 28:26–28). This interest in Isaiah may stem from the fact that Jesus quoted Isaiah 42:7, 16 when He spoke to Paul on the Damascus Road (Acts 26:16–18). When Jesus encouraged Paul during his ministry to Corinth (Acts. 18:9–10), He referred to Isaiah 41:10 and 43:5. Paul's call to evangelize the Gentiles was confirmed by Isaiah 49:6. Like the prophet Isaiah, Paul saw the vastness of God's plan for both Jews and Gentiles; and like Isaiah, Paul magnified Jesus Christ, the Savior of the world. Five times in his letters Paul referred to Isaiah 53.

As you study Isaiah and discover God's prophetic plan for the nations of the world, don't miss his emphasis on the personal message of God's forgiveness. "Though your sins be as scarlet, they shall be as white as snow; though they be red like crimson, they shall be as wool" (1:18). "I have blotted out, like a thick cloud, your transgressions, and, like a cloud, your sins" (44:22 NKJV). "I, even I, am He who blots out your transgressions for My own sake; and I will not remember your sins" (43:25 NKJV).

How can "the Holy One of Israel," a just and righteous God, forgive our sins and remember them no more?

"But [Jesus] was wounded for our transgressions, He was bruised for our iniquities; the chastisement for our peace was upon Him, and by His stripes we are healed" (53:5 NKJV).

It was on the basis of this truth that Peter declared, "To [Jesus] all the prophets witness that, through His name, whoever believes in Him will receive remission of sins" (Acts 10:43 NKJV).

"Who hath believed our report?" Isaiah asks us (53:1).

"If you will not believe, surely you shall not be established," he warns us (7:9 NKJV).

If you have never believed on the Lord Jesus Christ and received Him into your life, then do so now. "Look to Me, and be saved, all you ends of the earth! For I am God, and there is no other" (45:22 NKJV).

"Nor is there salvation in any other, for there is no other name under heaven given among men by which we must be saved" (Acts 4:12 NKJV).

# QUESTIONS FOR PERSONAL REFLECTION
# OR GROUP DISCUSSION

1. What leadership traits or characteristics do people expect of religious leaders today?

2. How do the traits you listed for question 1 compare or contrast with those of Isaiah?

3. What dangers was Judah (Isaiah's nation) facing?

4. G. Campbell Morgan describes Isaiah as "a man who spoke to an inattentive age." What personal needs for comfort might Isaiah have had?

5. As you look at the main divisions of Isaiah's book, which topics sound appealing to read about? Why those?

6. Why do you think Isaiah's audience might have been turned off by the first part of his message? How could it go against the grain of their expectations?

7. What is the value of reading prophecies of judgment? What is the value of reading prophecies of hope?

8. How can we effectively communicate to our culture about judgment (or is it impossible)? About hope?

9. What prophecies about the Messiah can you find in Isaiah?

10. Which of Isaiah's four "words"—warning, promise, hope, salvation—might God most want you to hear? Why that one?

# Chapter Two

# WANTED: A PROPHET

### (Isaiah 1—6)

The first thing you must know about prophets is that their ministry focuses on the present as well as on the future. They "tell forth" the Word of God as well as "foretell" the works of God. True prophets are like good doctors: They diagnose the case, prescribe a remedy, and warn the patient what will happen if the prescription is ignored (see Jer. 6:14; 8:11). When prophets declare a vision of the future, they do it to encourage people to obey God today. Peter stated this principle when he wrote, "Therefore, since all these things will be dissolved, what manner of persons ought you to be in holy conduct and godliness?" (2 Peter 3:11 NKJV).

Unlike Jeremiah and Ezekiel, Isaiah did not begin his book with an account of his call to ministry. This he gave in chapter 6. Instead, he started with a probing examination of Judah's present situation and gave a passionate plea for God's people to return to the Lord. As you read his analysis, note how closely it parallels our situation in the Western world.

## WHAT ISAIAH SAW (1:1–31)

This chapter describes a courtroom scene. God convenes the court and states the charges (vv. 2–4). He presents His case and pronounces the

prostitute, murderers
rebels, you do not defend
the fatherless

Sins of the ten commandments
God in the cloud on the mountain

nation guilty (vv. 5–15), but He gives the accused opportunity to repent and be forgiven (vv. 16–31). How did God describe His sinful people?

They were rebellious children (vv. 2–4) who did not have as much devotion to God as animals do to their masters! The word _rebel_ carries with it the idea of breaking a contract. At Sinai, Israel entered into a solemn covenant with Jehovah (Ex. 19—20), but they broke the contract with their unbelief and idolatry. They did not appreciate what God had done for them and were taking their blessings for granted. They had forsaken the Lord, gone backward, and grown corrupt; therefore, they were guilty and deserved judgment.

From the human point of view, the nation was prospering; but from God's point of view, the nation was like a wretched victim who had been beaten from head to foot and left to die (Isa. 1:5–6). The wounds had become infected, the whole body diseased, and nobody was doing anything to help. The false prophets and hypocritical priests of that day would have challenged Isaiah's autopsy of "the body politic," but the prophet knew that his diagnosis was true. In spite of the optimism of Judah's leaders, the nation was morally and spiritually sick, and judgment was inevitable.

In verses 7–9, God pictures Judah as a ravaged battlefield, a desert that had once been a garden. In using this image, Isaiah may have been looking ahead to the invasion of Sennacherib, when Judah was devastated by the Assyrian army and only Jerusalem was spared (chaps. 36—37). The people would not let God manage the land according to His law, so God turned Judah over to foreigners and permitted His people to suffer (Deut. 28:15ff.).

What a humiliating shock the people must have had when they heard Isaiah compare the Holy City of Jerusalem to the wicked cities of Sodom and Gomorrah (Isa. 3:9; Gen. 18—19)! And what did the leaders think when Isaiah said only "a very small remnant" would survive? After all, God promised Abraham that the nation would multiply like the dust of the earth and the stars of the heavens (Gen. 13:16; 15:5). The doctrine of "the remnant" is important in the message of the prophets (Isa. 6:13; 10:20–22; 11:11–13, 16; Jer. 6:9; 23:3; 31:7; Mic. 2:12; Zech. 8:12). Paul also referred to it (Rom. 9:27; 11:5). In spite of the apostasy of the nation, a remnant of true believers would be spared so that God's work could be accomplished through the Jewish nation.

The disgusting thing about this rebellious people is that they were also a religious people (Isa. 1:10–15). They attended the temple services and brought a multitude of sacrifices to the Lord, but their hearts were far from God and their worship was hypocritical. Sacrifices alone can never please God, for along with the outward observance, God wants inward obedience (1 Sam. 15:22), a broken heart (Ps. 51:17), and a godly walk (Mic. 6:6–8). Judah's worship of Jehovah was iniquity, not piety, and God was sick of it! Instead of lifting up "holy hands" in prayer (1 Tim. 2:8), their hands were stained with blood because of their many sins (Isa. 59:3; Ezek. 7:23).

But before passing judgment on worshippers in a bygone era, perhaps we should confess the sins of the "worshipping church" today. According to researcher George Barna, 93 percent of the households in the United States contain a Bible and more than 60 percent of the people surveyed claim to be religious, but we would never know this from the way people act. One Protestant church exists for every 550 adults in America, but does all this "religion" make much of a difference in our sinful society? Organized religion hasn't affected the nation's crime rate, the divorce rate, or the kind of "entertainment" seen in movies and on TV.

The average church allocates about 5 percent of its budget for reaching others with the gospel, but 30 percent for buildings and maintenance. At a time when the poor and the aged are pleading for help, churches in America are spending approximately 3 billion dollars a year on new construction. Where churches have life and growth, such construction may be needed, but too often the building becomes "a millstone instead of a milestone," to quote Vance Havner. At least 62 percent of the people Barna surveyed said that the church was not relevant to today's world and is losing its influence on society. It may be that, like the worshippers in the ancient Jewish temple, we are only going through the motions. (See *The Frog in the Kettle* by George Barna, Regal, 1990.)

Isaiah didn't stop with the diagnosis but also gave the prescription, because he wanted Judah to be a righteous people (Isa. 1:16–31). The word translated "reason" in verse 18 means "to decide a case in court," but instead of pronouncing judgment, the Judge offered pardon! If they would cleanse themselves by repenting and turning from sin (vv. 16–17; see 2 Cor. 7:1), then God would wipe the record clean in response to their faith (Isa. 1:18). God had every reason to punish His people for their sins, but in His grace and mercy He offered them His pardon.

What were some of the sins that the nation needed to confess and put away? Isaiah named murder (v. 21), robbery, bribery, exploiting the helpless (v. 23), and the worship of heathen idols (v. 29). Because of their idolatry, the once-faithful wife was now a harlot, and because of their unjust practices, the pure silver had become dross. The tragedy is that many of the worshippers in the temple participated in these evil practices and thereby encouraged the decay of the nation. The rulers maintained a religious façade to cover up their crimes, and the people let them do it.

What would God do if the people did not repent? He would send a fiery judgment that would purge the dross and burn up those whose rebellion had made them His enemies (vv. 24–31). Isaiah closed this first message with a promise of hope that one day Jerusalem would be a "city of righteousness."

## WHAT ISAIAH PROMISED (2:1—4:6)

Three important phrases sum up Isaiah's second message and its proclamation of God's future work.

**(1) The temple of the Lord (2:1–5).** The prophet looked ahead to the time when God's righteous kingdom would be established and the temple would become the center for the worldwide worship of the Lord. In Isaiah's day, the Jews were adopting the false gods of the Gentiles, but the day would come when the Gentiles would abandon their idols and worship the true God of Israel. The nations would also lay down their weapons and stop warring. These promises must not be "spiritualized" and applied to the church, for they describe a literal kingdom of righteousness and peace. The Jewish temple will be rebuilt, and the Word of God will go forth from Jerusalem to govern the nations of the world.

In the light of the future glory of God's temple, Isaiah appealed to the people to "walk in the light of the LORD" (v. 5). Christians today have a similar motivation as we await the return of Christ for His church (1 John 2:28–3:3).

**(2) The day of the Lord (2:6—3:26).** This is that period of time when God will send judgment to the nations and purify Israel in preparation for the coming of His King to reign in Jerusalem. The day of the Lord is described by John (Rev. 6—19), by the prophets (Isa. 13:6ff.; Ezek. 30; Joel 1:15; 2:1ff.; Zeph. 1:7ff.; Zech. 14:1ff.), and by the Lord Jesus (Matt. 24; Mark 13; Luke 21). It will be a time of terrible suffering, the environment will be devastated, and millions of people will die. (Note the repetition of the phrase "in that day": Isa. 2:17, 20; 3:7, 18; 4:1–2.)

To the prophets, "the day of the Lord" was foreshadowed by events in their own day. In the book of Isaiah, Assyria's conquest of the northern kingdom and invasion of Judah, and the Babylonian captivity of Judah both picture the coming "day of the Lord."

*Why will God judge His people?* Because of their idolatry, covetousness, pride, and exploiting of the poor (2:6–22). Instead of holding to the truth of God's Word, they were adopting "superstitions from the East" (v. 6 NIV), not unlike many "religious seekers" today. The growth of Eastern religions in the modern Western world is a phenomenon that is both frightening and challenging. Even nonreligious people are practicing Eastern forms of meditation and relaxation, following techniques that are being taught in university classes and business seminars.

The prosperity of the nation made leaders proud and covetous. Instead of trusting the Lord, they trusted their wealth and war equipment, not realizing that neither would deliver them in the coming day of judgment. The leaders were exploiting the poor, crushing them like grain in a mill (3:13–15). God will not allow His people to be proud and self-confident, but will humble them and cut them down like trees in the forest. "The LORD alone shall be exalted in that day" (2:11, 17) when men flee from His wrath and discover the worthlessness of their idols and the consequences of their sins (vv. 19–22).

*How will God judge His people?* By taking away from them everything they were trusting, including food and water, leaders and soldiers, and judges and prophets (3:1–15). The entire support system of the nation would disintegrate, and there would be no remedy. Nobody would want to hold office except women and children. (In Judah's male-dominated society, this would be a humiliating calamity.) The national leaders in Isaiah's day were charting a course that was out of the will of God and would ultimately bring disaster, but the righteous remnant would be protected by God (vv. 10–12).

After denouncing the men in leadership, the prophet zeroed in on the proud women who profited from their husbands' crimes (3:16—4:1). The prophet Amos had a similar message for the women in the northern kingdom (Amos 4:1–3). Everything would be different for these women when the judgment of God came to the land! In that day, nobody would notice their expensive clothes, their jewelry and perfumes, and their elaborate coiffures. They would be prisoners of war, led by a rope, like cattle going to the slaughter. So many men would be killed there wouldn't be enough husbands to go around (4:1)!

God is longsuffering as He watches people viciously exploit one another and selfishly ravage His creation. But there is coming a day when unbelieving sinners will be punished and God's people will share in the glories of His kingdom. Are you ready?

**(3) The Branch of the Lord (4:2–6).** The prophet looked beyond the "day of the Lord" to that time when the kingdom will be established on earth. "Branch of the Lord" is a messianic title for Jesus Christ, who came as a "shoot" from the seeming dead stump of David's dynasty (11:1; 53:2; see Jer. 23:5; 33:15; Zech. 3:8; 6:12). God will cleanse His people (Isa. 4:4; see Zech. 12:10—13:1), restore the fruitfulness of the land, and dwell with them as He did when He led them through the wilderness (Isa. 4:5–6; Ex. 13:21–22). Not just the temple, but every dwelling will be blessed by the presence of the Lord! Unlike in Isaiah's day, "in that day" the people will be holy (set apart), and the land will be beautiful and glorious.

## WHAT ISAIAH SANG (5:1–30)

The preacher became a troubadour and sang a folk song to the Lord ("my beloved"). Perhaps the people who had ignored his sermons would listen to his song. He sang about his own people (v. 7) and pointed out how good God had been to them. God gave them a holy law and a wonderful land, but they broke the law and defiled the land with their sins and failed to produce fruit for God's glory. God had done for them all that He could do. Now all that remained for Him to do was bring judgment on the fruitless vineyard and make it a waste. (Note that Jesus referred to this passage in Matt. 21:33–44.)

What were the "wild grapes" that the nation produced instead of the "good grapes" that God sought for? In the six "woes" that follow, Isaiah named the sins that brought judgment on the land.

**(1) Covetousness (vv. 8–10).** In disobedience to the law (Lev. 25:23–28; 1 Kings 21:1–3), the rich defrauded the poor and seized the land. These wealthy exploiters built large mansions and developed extensive farms, but God warned them that their houses would be empty and their harvests meager. Imagine ten acres of grapevines yielding only six gallons of wine and six bushels of seed producing half a bushel of grain!

(2) **Drunkenness (vv. 11–17).** In the Old Testament, God did not require total abstinence, but He did warn against drunkenness (Prov. 20:1; 23:29–31; Hab. 2:15). This warning is repeated in the New Testament for believers today (Rom. 13:13; 1 Cor. 6:9–10; Eph. 5:18). Isaiah described people so addicted to alcohol that they begin their revelries as soon as they wake up in the morning, and they continue their drinking till late at night. They enjoy banquets and music and get involved in drunken brawls (Isa. 5:14 NIV). But when judgment comes, these people will hunger and thirst and become "food" for the grave (v. 14). The "eaters" will themselves be eaten, and the proud drinkers will be brought low.

(3) **Carelessness (vv. 18–19).** Isaiah described people who are bound by sin and yet speak frequently of the Lord and His warnings. "They even mock the Holy One of Israel and dare the Lord to punish them" (v. 19 TLB). The name "Holy One of Israel" is used twenty-five times in Isaiah, but these sinners had no respect for that name. We have skeptical scoffers today who speak lightly of the Lord and think they will get away with it.

(4) **Deception (v. 20).** Moral standards were destroyed by new definitions of sin (see Amos 5:7), people using God's vocabulary but not His dictionary. Like today's "double-speak," this kind of language made it easy to deceive people and avoid a guilty conscience. In today's world, increased taxes are "revenue enhancements," and poor people are "fiscal underachievers." Medical malpractice is not the cause of a patient's death; it's a "diagnostic misadventure of high magnitude" (see *DoubleSpeak* by William Lutz). The Jerusalem Bible translation of Psalm 12:2 says it perfectly: "All they do is lie to one another, flattering lips, talk from a double heart."

**(5) Pride (v. 21).** Instead of listening to God, the leaders consulted with one another and made decisions based on their own wisdom. "Professing themselves to be wise, they became fools" (Rom. 1:22; see 1 Cor. 1:18–25). "Do not be wise in your own eyes; fear the LORD and depart from evil" (Prov. 3:7 NKJV).

**(6) Injustice (vv. 22–25).** The judges who were supposed to enforce the law used their authority to free the guilty and punish the innocent. They were more interested in cocktail parties than fair trials, and making money (bribes) than promoting justice. Isaiah warned these corrupt politicians that the fire of God's wrath was coming and would burn them up. They were like cut flowers and had no roots, beautiful for a time, but destined to die and turn to dust.

The phrase in verse 25 about God's anger is repeated in 9:12, 17, 21, and 10:4. His hand was raised in judgment and would not come down until He had completed His work. He would summon the Assyrian army from afar and use it to chasten His people (5:26–30). The northern kingdom of Israel would be destroyed, and Judah, the southern kingdom, would be devastated but eventually delivered, only to go in captivity to Babylon a century later. God was serious about the nation's sins. If they would not repent and accept His offer of pardon (1:18), then all He could do was send judgment.

## WHAT ISAIAH EXPERIENCED (6:1–13)

Anyone reading Isaiah's first two messages might be inclined to ask, "What right does this man have to pronounce judgment on the leaders of our land and the many worshippers in the temple?" The answer is in this chapter: Isaiah's account of his call to ministry. Before he announced any "woes" on others, he first confessed his own sin and said, "Woe is me!" He saw the Holy One of Israel, and he could not keep silent. Note four stages in Isaiah's experience with God.

**(1) Sight: He saw the Lord (vv. 1–4).** We assume that Isaiah was in the temple when this marvelous event occurred, but we cannot be sure. The temple referred to in verse 1 is the heavenly temple, rather than Solomon's temple. King Uzziah died in 740 BC and was one of Judah's greatest leaders, even though in his latter years he was disciplined for disobeying God (2 Chron. 26:16–21). A great king may have left his throne on earth, but the greatest King was still seated on the throne of heaven. According to John 12:41, this was the Lord Jesus Christ.

Only here are the seraphim mentioned in Scripture. The Hebrew word means "to burn" and relates these creatures to the holiness of God. This is why they repeat "Holy, holy, holy" before the throne of God. Some students think that the seraphim are the "living creatures" described in Revelation 4:6–9.

When I was the radio speaker on "Songs in the Night" from the Moody Church in Chicago, I often received clippings from listeners, items they thought might be useful on the weekly broadcast. Most of them I have forgotten, but a few of them still stick in my mind. One of the best was, "When the outlook is bleak, try the uplook!"

For young Isaiah, the outlook was bleak. His beloved king had died, his nation was in peril, and he could do very little about it. The outlook may have been bleak, but the uplook was glorious! God was still on the throne and reigning as the Sovereign of the universe! From heaven's point of view, "the whole earth" was "full of his glory" (Isa. 6:3; see Num. 14:21–22; Ps. 72:18–19). When your world tumbles in, it is good to look at things from heaven's point of view.

**(2) Insight: He saw himself (vv. 5–7).** The sight of a holy God and the sound of the holy hymn of worship brought great conviction to Isaiah's heart, and he confessed that he was a sinner. Unclean lips are caused by an unclean heart (Matt. 12:34–35). Isaiah cried out to be cleansed inwardly (Ps. 51:10), and God met his need. If this scene had been on earth, the coals would have come from the brazen altar where sacrificial blood had been shed, or perhaps from the censer of the high priest on the Day of Atonement (Lev. 16:12). Isaiah's cleansing came by blood and fire, and it was verified by the word of the Lord (Isa. 6:7).

Before we can minister to others, we must permit God to minister to us. Before we pronounce "woe" upon others, we must sincerely say, "Woe is me!" Isaiah's conviction led to confession, and confession led to cleansing (1 John 1:9). Like Isaiah, many of the great heroes of faith saw themselves as sinners and humbled themselves before God: Abraham (Gen. 18:27), Jacob (32:10), Job (Job 40:1–5), David (2 Sam. 7:18), Paul (1 Tim. 1:15), and Peter (Luke 5:8–11).

**(3) Vision: He saw the need (v. 8).** The nation needed the Lord, and the Lord wanted a servant to minister to the people. Isaiah volunteered to be that servant. He did not discuss his call with the Lord, as did Moses (Ex. 3:11—4:15) and Jeremiah (Jer. 1:4ff.), but accepted the appointment and made himself available to his Master.

Never underestimate what God can do with one willing worker. There is an even greater need for laborers today, and we have tremendous opportunities for sharing the gospel with a lost world. Are you one of God's willing volunteers?

**(4) Blindness: The nation could not see (vv. 9–13).** The Lord did not give His servant much encouragement! Isaiah's ministry would actually make some people's eyes more blind, their ears more deaf, and their hearts more callused. Verses 9–10 are so important that they are quoted six times in the New Testament (Matt. 13:13–15; Mark 4:12; Luke 8:10; John 12:40; Acts 28:25–28; Rom. 11:8). God does not deliberately make sinners blind, deaf, and hard-hearted; but the more that people resist God's truth, the less able they are to receive God's truth. But the servant is to proclaim the Word no matter how people respond, for the test of ministry is not outward success but faithfulness to the Lord.

God told Isaiah that his ministry would end in seeming failure, with the land ruined and the people taken off to exile (Isa. 6:11–12). But a remnant would survive! It would be like the stump of a fallen tree from which the shoots ("the holy seed") would come, and they would continue the true faith in the land. Isaiah needed a long-range perspective on his ministry or else he would feel like he was accomplishing nothing.

"Go and tell" is still God's command to His people (v. 9; see Matt. 28:7; Mark 5:19). He is waiting for us to reply, "Here am I; send me."

# QUESTIONS FOR PERSONAL REFLECTION OR GROUP DISCUSSION

1. When hypocrisy or scandals in the church are well-known, how can the church regain credibility? What practical expression of repentance might the church demonstrate?

2. How does God describe His people in Isaiah 1? Talk about the meaning of the imagery He uses.

3. What were the four stages in Isaiah's experience of God (6:1–13)? Which of these do you recognize as being neglected in your own life?

4. How does a call for repentance spell hope for those who've gone astray?

5. Isaiah's message to his culture included the carrot (promises of hope) and stick (warnings of judgment). How effective do you think this approach would be in motivating those in our culture who have strayed from God's standard? What makes you say that?

6. Why did Isaiah use music (5:1–30) as a creative medium to call people to repentance?

7. To whom was the song sung? About whom was it sung (see Isa. 5:1)?

8. Read the lyrics of Isaiah's song. What does he say about greed and materialism?

9. Why do you suppose Isaiah was so concerned about people's use of money and their treatment of the poor? What relevance does this emphasis have for us today?

10. How did Jesus refer to this song to address another generation (see Matt. 21:33–44)?

11. What title would you give Isaiah's song, and why?

# Chapter Three

# GOD IS WITH US!

## (Isaiah 7—12)

B ehold, I and the children whom the LORD hath given me are for signs and for wonders in Israel from the LORD of hosts" (Isa. 8:18).

This statement by the prophet Isaiah is a key to understanding the meaning of the events and prophecies in this section. In his previous messages, Isaiah focused on the spiritual needs of his people, but in this section he deals with the political situation and the failure of the leaders to trust the Lord. Four symbolic names are involved in Isaiah's messages, each of them with a very special meaning: Emmanuel, Maher-shalal-hash-baz, Shear-jashub, and Isaiah.

### EMMANUEL: A MESSAGE OF HOPE (7:1–25)

**A promise to King Ahaz (vv. 1–9).** These were perilous days for the nation of Judah. Assyria was growing stronger and threatening the smaller nations whose security depended on a very delicate political balance. Syria and Ephraim (the northern kingdom) tried to pressure Judah into an alliance against Assyria, but Ahaz refused to join them. Why? Because he had secretly made a treaty with Assyria (2 Kings 16:5–9)! The king was playing "power politics" instead of trusting in the power of God. Syria and Ephraim planned to overthrow Ahaz and put "the son of Tabeel" on the throne, and Ahaz was a frightened man.

The Lord commanded Isaiah to take his son Shear-jashub ("a remnant shall return") and meet Ahaz as the king was inspecting the city's water system. Ahaz's heart had been wavering, and the hearts of his people had been shaking for fear (Isa. 7:2), but Isaiah came with a message of assurance: "Take heed, and be quiet; fear not, neither be fainthearted" (v. 4). How would Ahaz find this inner peace? By believing God's promise that Judah's enemies would be defeated. "If you will not believe, surely you shall not be established" (v. 9 NKJV). Faith in God's promises is the only way to find peace in the midst of trouble. "You will keep him in perfect peace, whose mind is stayed on You, because he trusts in You" (26:3 NKJV).

In God's eyes, the two threatening kings were nothing but "two smoldering stubs of firewood" (7:4 NIV) who would be off the scene very soon, and they both died two years later. Furthermore, within sixty-five years, Ephraim (Israel, the northern kingdom) would be gone forever. Isaiah spoke this prophecy in the year 734 BC. Assyria defeated Syria in 732 BC and invaded Israel in 722 BC. They deported many of the Jews and assimilated the rest by introducing Gentiles into the land. By 669 BC (sixty-five years later), the nation no longer existed.

**A sign to the house of David (vv. 10–16).** If Ahaz had believed God's promise, he would have broken his alliance and called the nation to prayer and praise, but the king continued in his unbelief. Realizing the weakness of the king's faith, Isaiah offered to give a sign to encourage him, but Ahaz put on a "pious front" and refused his offer. Knowing that he was secretly allied with Assyria, how could Ahaz honestly ask the Lord for a special sign? So, instead of speaking only to the king, Isaiah addressed the whole "house of David" and gave the prophecy concerning "Emmanuel."

Of course, the ultimate fulfillment of this prophecy is in our Lord
Jesus Christ, who is "God with us" (Matt. 1:18–25; Luke 1:31–35). The
virgin birth of Christ is a key doctrine; for if Jesus Christ is not God come
in sinless human flesh, then we have no Savior. Jesus had to be born of
a virgin, apart from human generation, because He existed before His
mother. He was not just born in this world; He came down from heaven
into the world (John 3:13; 6:33, 38, 41–42, 50–51, 58). Jesus was sent by
the Father and therefore came into the world having a human mother but
not a human father (4:34; 5:23–24, 30; 9:4).

However, this "sign" had an immediate significance to Ahaz and the
people of Judah. A woman who was then a virgin would get married, con-
ceive, and bear a son whose name would be "Emmanuel." The son would
be a reminder that God was with His people and would care for them. It is
likely that this virgin was Isaiah's second wife—his first wife having died
after Shear-jasub was born—and that Isaiah's second son was named both
"Emmanuel" and "Maher-shalal-hash-baz" (8:1–4; note vv. 8, 10).

Orthodox Jewish boys become "sons of the law" at the age of twelve.
This special son was a reminder that Syria and Ephraim would be out of
the picture within the next twelve years. Isaiah delivered his prophecy in
734 BC. In 732 BC Assyria defeated Syria, and in 722 BC Assyria invaded
the northern kingdom. The prophecy was fulfilled.

**A warning to Judah (vv. 17–25).** Instead of trusting the Lord, Ahaz
continued to trust Assyria for help, and Isaiah warned him that Assyria
would become Judah's enemy. The Assyrians would invade Judah and so
ravage the land that agriculture would cease and the people would have
only dairy products to eat (vv. 15, 21–23). The rich farmland would
become wasteland, and the people would be forced to hunt wild beasts in
order to get food. It would be a time of great humiliation (v. 20; 2 Sam.
10:4–5) and suffering that could have been avoided had the leaders trusted
in the Lord.

## MAHER-SHALAL-HASH-BAZ: A WARNING OF JUDGMENT (8:1–22)

Isaiah married the virgin, and the legal documents were duly witnessed and sealed. He even announced that their first child would be a son and his name would be Maher-shalal-hash-baz, which means "quick to plunder, swift to the spoil." Since Isaiah's sons were signs to the nation (8:18), this name was significant. It spoke of future judgment when Assyria would conquer Syria and invade both Israel and Judah, and when Babylon would take Judah into exile. A child would start speaking meaningful sentences about the age of two. In 732 BC, about two years after Isaiah's son was born, both Pekah and Rezin were dead (7:1), and Assyria had conquered Syria and begun to invade Israel (2 Kings 15:29). The army was "quick to plunder and swift to take the spoil."

In the remainder of this chapter, Isaiah used three vivid contrasts to show the rulers of Judah the mistake they were making by trusting Assyria instead of trusting the Lord.

**(1) They chose a flood instead of a peaceful river (vv. 8:5–10).** The pro-Assyrian faction in Judah rejoiced when Assyria defeated Syria and when both Pekah and Rezin died. These victories seemed to prove that an alliance with Assyria was the safest course to follow. Instead of trusting the Lord ("the waters of Shiloah that go softly" in v. 6), they trusted the great river of Assyria. What they did not realize was that this river would become a flood when Assyria would come and destroy Israel and devastate Judah. God offered His people peace, but in unbelief they opted for war. They were walking by sight and not by faith.

But Isaiah saw no permanent victory for the invading army. After all, they were entering Emmanuel's land, and God was with His people and would deliver them for His name's sake. Assyria might plan its strategy, but God would thwart its every move. Sennacherib's army camped around Jerusalem, certain of victory, but God wiped them out with a single blow (chap. 37).

**(2) They chose a snare instead of a sanctuary (vv. 8:11–15).** God warned Isaiah not to follow the majority and support the popular pro-Assyrian party. Even though his stand was looked upon as treason, Isaiah opposed all foreign alliances and urged the people to put their faith in the Lord (7:9; 28:16; 30:15). The Jewish political leaders were asking, "Is it popular? Is it safe?" But the prophet was asking, "Is it right? Is it the will of God?"

When you fear the Lord, you don't need to fear people or circumstances. Peter referred to this passage when he wrote, "But even if you should suffer for what is right, you are blessed. 'Do not fear what they fear; do not be frightened.' But in your hearts set apart Christ as Lord" (1 Peter 3:14–15 NIV). Isaiah compared the Lord to a sanctuary, a rock that is a refuge for believers but a snare to those who rebel. The image of Messiah as a rock is found again in Isaiah 28:16 (and see 1 Peter 2:4–7; Rom. 9:33). "God is our refuge and strength, a very present help in trouble" (Ps. 46:1).

**(3) They chose darkness instead of light (vv. 16–22).** The nation had rejected Isaiah's message, but that didn't mean that his ministry was a failure. The true disciples of the Lord received God's Word and treasured it in their hearts. By faith, the prophet was willing to wait patiently for God's Word to be fulfilled.

But even if his words fell on deaf ears, Isaiah and his family were themselves a "living prophecy" that the nation could not ignore. Isaiah's name means "Jehovah is salvation," and this would remind the people to trust the Lord to deliver them. His older son's name means "A remnant shall return," and this was a word of promise when it looked as though the nation was destroyed. A believing remnant did return to Jerusalem from Babylon, and they were encouraged by what Isaiah wrote in chapters 40—66. The name of the younger son, Maher-shalal-hash-baz, means "quick to plunder, swift to the spoil," and pointed to the fall of Syria and Ephraim. Verse 18 is quoted in Hebrews 2:13–14 and applied to the Lord Jesus Christ.

In their time of crisis, instead of turning to God for wisdom, the people consulted demons (Isa. 8:19; Deut. 18:10–12), and this only increased their moral and spiritual darkness. The increase of the occult in our own day is evidence that people are deliberately rejecting God's Word and turning to Satan's lies. "If they do not speak according to this word, they have no light of dawn" (Isa. 8:20 NIV). Judah's leaders anxiously looked for the dawning of a new day, but they saw only a deepening darkness. God's Word is our only dependable light in this world's darkness (Ps. 119:105; 2 Peter 1:19–21).

## SHEAR-JASHUB: A PROMISE OF MERCY (9:1—11:16)

This name means "A remnant shall return," and the return of the Jewish remnant to their land is a major theme in these chapters (10:20–22; 11:11–12, 16). When Assyria conquered the northern kingdom of Israel (Ephraim), the nation was never restored but became what we know as Samaria. After the Babylonian captivity (606–586 BC), the people of Judah were given another chance to establish themselves in the land, and through them the Lord brought the Messiah into the world. Had a remnant not returned, God's plans for redeeming a lost world might have been frustrated. How much depended on that small remnant!

God's mercy to His people is seen in four ministries the Lord performed for them.

**(1) The Lord promised them a Redeemer (9:1–7).** Isaiah continued the theme of light and darkness (8:20–22) by announcing, "There will be no more gloom" (9:1 NIV). The Redeemer will come and bring to the world the dawning of a new day (v. 2; Luke 1:78–79; John 8:12). We know that this prophecy refers to Christ because of the way it is quoted in Matthew 4:13–15. The geographical areas named in Isaiah 9:1 were especially devastated when the Assyrian army moved in, but these areas would be especially honored by the ministry of the Messiah. Jesus was identified with "Galilee of the Gentiles" (Matt. 4:15 NIV), and His loving ministry to the people brought light and joy.

But the prophet looked beyond the first coming of Christ to His second coming and the establishing of His righteous kingdom (Isa. 9:3–7). Instead of protecting a small remnant, God would enlarge the nation. Instead of experiencing sorrow, the people would rejoice like reapers after a great harvest, soldiers after a great victory, or prisoners of war after being released from their yoke of bondage. Of course, some of this occurred when God defeated Assyria and delivered Jerusalem (Isa. 37). But the ultimate fulfillment is still future; all military material will be destroyed (9:5) because the nations will not learn war any more (2:4).

Isaiah 9:6 declared both the humanity ("a Child is born") and the deity ("a Son is given") of the Lord Jesus Christ. The prophet then leaps ahead to the kingdom age, when the Messiah will reign in righteousness and justice from David's throne. God had promised David that his dynasty and throne would be established forever (2 Sam. 7:16), and this is fulfilled literally in Jesus Christ (Luke 1:32–33; Zech. 9:9), who will one day reign from Jerusalem (Isa. 11:1–5; Jer. 23:5–8; 30:8–10). This kingdom is called "the millennium," which means "one thousand years." The phrase is used six times in Revelation 20.

If His name is "Wonderful," then there will be nothing dull about His reign! As Counselor, He has the wisdom to rule justly; and as the Mighty God, He has the power to execute His wise plans. "Everlasting Father" does not suggest that the Son is also the Father, for each Person in the Godhead is distinct. "Father of eternity" is a better translation. Among the Jews, the word *father* means "originator" or "source." For example, Satan is the "father [originator] of lies" (John 8:44 NIV). If you want anything eternal, you must get it from Jesus Christ; He is the "Father of eternity."

**(2) The Lord judged Israel for their sins (9:8—10:4).** This long section describes what will happen to the northern kingdom when the Assyrians invade. While Isaiah's ministry was primarily to the people of Judah, he used Israel as an object lesson to warn the southern kingdom that

God does not take sin lightly. Judah had sinned greatly, but God in His mercy spared them for David's sake (37:35; 1 Kings 11:13; 15:4; 2 Chron. 21:7). However, God's longsuffering would one day end.

The key statement is "For all this his anger is not turned away, but his hand is stretched out still" (Isa. 9:12, 17, 21; 10:4; and see 5:25). This is the outstretched hand of God's judgment, not His mercy (65:2; Rom. 10:21). God judged them for their pride in thinking that their present difficulties were temporary and the nation could rebuild itself better than before (Isa. 9:8–12). He also judged them for their hardness of heart in their refusal to repent and return to the Lord (vv. 13–17). God's loving purpose in chastening is that we yield to Him, but if we harden our hearts, then chastening becomes judgment (Heb. 12:1–11). Israel was being led astray by false prophets and foolish leaders; the nation would not listen to God's Word.

Ephraim's own wickedness was destroying the nation the way a fire destroys a forest or a field (Isa. 9:18–19). But the sinners would become fuel for the fire God could kindle! In their greed, the people of the northern kingdom were devouring one another (v. 20) and battling one another (v. 21), but they would soon be devoured and defeated by Assyria.

In 10:1–4, Isaiah denounced Ephraim for its injustice, especially toward the poor, the widows, and the orphans. Unjust laws and oppressive decrees robbed these people both of their meager possessions and their God-given rights (Deut. 15:7–8; 24:17–18). The prophet's three questions in Isaiah 10:3 ought to be pondered by every person who wants to be ready when the Lord comes.

If God cannot bring us to repentance through His Word, then He must lift His hand and chasten us. If we do not submit to His chastening, then He must stretch out His hand and judge us. God is longsuffering, but we dare not tempt Him by our careless or callous attitude. "It is a fearful thing to fall into the hands of the living God" (Heb. 10:31).

**(3) The Lord will judge the enemy (10:5–34).** "Woe to the Assyrian!" is the way this section begins (see NIV). Though God used Assyria to chasten Judah, He would not permit His "tool" to exalt itself in pride. Assyria was His rod, club, axe, and saw (10:5, 15, 24), but the Assyrians treated the Jews like mud in the streets (v. 6) and plundered the land like a farmer gathering eggs (v. 14). God's purpose was to discipline, but the Assyrians were out to destroy (v. 7). They boasted of their conquests (vv. 8–14; see 37:10–13) but did not give glory to God.

Because of their arrogant attitude, God would judge Assyria, for the worker certainly has mastery over His tools! Like a wasting disease and a blazing forest fire, God's wrath would come to this proud nation and its army. He would cut them down like trees in the forest (10:33–34). In the days of Hezekiah, God wiped out 185,000 of the Assyrian soldiers (37:36–37), and the great Assyrian Empire ultimately fell to Babylon in 609 BC.

In spite of Assyria's conquest of the northern kingdom and its intention to destroy Judah, God would save a remnant so that "the twelve tribes" would not be annihilated (Acts 26:7; James 1:1; Rev. 21:12). "The remnant shall return" (Isa. 10:21) is the translation of the name of Isaiah's older son, Shear-jashub.

In verses 28–32, Isaiah traces the advance of the Assyrian army as it invaded Judah and marched toward Jerusalem. But God's word to the people was "O My people that dwellest in Zion, be not afraid of the Assyrian" (v. 24)! Isaiah gave the same message to King Hezekiah when the Assyrian army surrounded Jerusalem in 701 BC (37:1–7). God used Assyria to discipline His people, but He would not permit this godless nation to go beyond His purposes. God may use unbelievers to accomplish His will in the lives of His people, but He is always in control. We need never fear the disciplining hand of God, for He always disciplines in love (Heb. 12:1–11).

**(4) The Lord will restore His people (11:1–16).** In contrast to the proud trees that God cuts down (10:33–34) is a tender shoot from a seemingly dead stump. Isaiah looked beyond his people's trials to the glorious kingdom that will be established when the Messiah comes to reign (11:1–9). David's dynasty was ready to end, but out of his family the Messiah would come (Rom. 1:3; Rev. 5:5). A godly remnant of Jews kept the nation alive so that the Messiah could be born.

His kingdom will involve righteous rule (Isa. 11:1–5) because the Son of God and the Spirit of God will administer its affairs justly. When the Messiah-King speaks the word, it is with power (Ps. 2:9; Rev. 19:15). His kingdom will also mean a restored creation because nature will once again enjoy the harmony it enjoyed before sin entered in (Isa. 11:6–9; Rom. 8:18–25). "The earth shall be full of the knowledge of the LORD, as the waters cover the sea" (Isa. 11:9; see Heb. 2:14).

The nucleus of the kingdom will be a regathered and reunited Jewish nation (Isa. 11:10–16). The "Root" will become a "banner" for the rallying of the people as the Lord reaches out and gathers His people from the nations where they have been exiled (43:5–6). It will be like a "second exodus" as God opens the way for His people to return to their land. In a limited sense, this promise was fulfilled after the Assyrian conquest and when the Jews left Babylonian captivity, but the ultimate fulfillment will be at the end of the age when the Messiah regathers His people (27:12–13; 49:22–23; 56:7–8; Matt. 24:31; Rom. 11:25–29). The centuries-long division between Israel and Judah will come to an end, and even the Gentiles will walk on "the highway" that leads to Jerusalem.

The "highway" is one of Isaiah's favorite images. Those who obey the Lord have a level and smooth road to walk (Isa. 26:7–8). When God calls His people back to their land, He will prepare the way for them (40:3–4) and lead them safely (42:16). He will remove obstacles so the people can travel easily (49:11; 57:14; 62:10). God's highway will be called "The way of holiness" (35:8).

When Isaiah looked at his people he saw a sinful nation that would one day walk the "highway of holiness" and enter into a righteous kingdom. He saw a suffering people who would one day enjoy a beautiful and peaceful kingdom. He saw a scattered people who would be regathered and reunited under the kingship of Jesus Christ. Jesus taught us to pray, "Thy kingdom come" (Matt. 6:10); for only when His kingdom comes can there be peace on earth.

## ISAIAH: A SONG OF SALVATION (12:1–6)

Isaiah's name means "Jehovah is salvation," and "salvation" is a key theme in this song. "In that day" refers to the day of Israel's regathering and reunion and the righteous reign of the Lord Jesus Christ. The Jewish remnant will have come through the time of tribulation on earth ("the time of Jacob's trouble," Jer. 30:7), seen their Messiah, repented, and received Him by faith (Zech. 12:10—13:1; 14:4–11). Cleansed and established in their promised kingdom, the nation will praise the Lord and extol Him among the Gentiles.

The refrain in Isaiah 12:2 ("The LORD JEHOVAH is my strength and my song; he also is become my salvation") was sung at the Exodus (Ex. 15:2) and at the rededication of the temple in Ezra's day (Ps. 118:14). It was sung by the Red Sea after the Jews had been delivered from Egypt by Moses, a prophet. It was sung in Jerusalem when the second temple was dedicated under the leadership of Ezra, a priest. It will be sung again when the Jewish nation accepts Jesus Christ as its King. They will recognize Him as "the Holy One of Israel" and willingly obey His holy law.

This joyful song closes this section of Isaiah in which the prophet has used four significant names to tell the people what God had planned for them. Because of Emmanuel, there is a message of hope.

Maher-shalal-hash-baz gives a warning of judgment, but his brother, Shear-jashub, speaks of a promise of mercy. The father's name, Isaiah, brings a song of rejoicing as the people discover that Jehovah is indeed their salvation.

The Lord will never forsake His people. No matter how difficult the days may be, or how long the nights, for the people of God, the best is yet to come.

# QUESTIONS FOR PERSONAL REFLECTION
# OR GROUP DISCUSSION

1. Even though there are positive aspects to independence, how can self-reliance become sin?

2. In what way was Ahaz tempted to play "power politics" rather than trust in God? How did God's perspective differ from Ahaz's?

God is with us?

3. What is the meaning of the name *Emmanuel?* What was its significance in Isaiah's day? In our day?

4. How did trusting Assyria rather than trusting the Lord bring judgment? In what ways did their trust backfire? What lessons in this story are there for us today?

5. In Isaiah 10:12–19, what surprise is there for Assyria?

I will punish the king of Assyria for the willful pride of his heart

6. How does the doctrine of the remnant give hope (see Isa. 10:20–22)?

7. How does God give His people a future? What are the characteristics of that future (see Isa. 9:1–7; 11:1–10)?

8. What can we learn about Christ from these chapters? For example, what crucial truth do we learn about Him from the dual statement, "a child is born" and "a Son is given"?

9. Over and over, these prophecies speak of justice. Christ will ultimately rule with justice. How important is it for us now to be pursuers of justice? Why?

10. For what does Isaiah praise God in 12:1–6? Can you praise God for similar things? Explain.

# Chapter Four

# THE BURDENED PROPHET

## (Isaiah 13—23)

"W hether you like it or not, history is on our side. We will bury you!"

The premier of the Soviet Union, Nikita Khrushchev, made that statement to a group of Western diplomats on November 18, 1956. But Khrushchev is dead, and the Soviet Union no longer exists. Khrushchev's boastful prophecy was not fulfilled.

Is there a pattern to history? Is anyone in charge? The British historian Edward Gibbon called history "little more than the register of crimes, follies, and misfortunes of mankind." But the American missionary leader Arthur T. Pierson said that "history is His story." Which one is right?

The prophet Isaiah would stand with Pierson, for these eleven chapters are certainly evidence that God is at work in the nations of the world. In these chapters, the prophet revealed God's plan not only for Judah, but also for ten Gentile nations. President James Garfield called history "the unrolled scroll of prophecy," and Isaiah unrolled the scroll for us to read.

World leaders need to learn the lesson that Nebuchadnezzar learned the hard way, that "the Most High rules in the kingdom of men, and gives it to whomever He chooses" (Dan. 4:25 NKJV). Paul made the same declaration to the Greek philosophers in Athens: "[God] determined the times set for [the nations] and the exact places where they should live" (Acts 17:26 NIV). Indeed, "history is His story."

Isaiah called these prophetic declarations "burdens" (Isa. 13:1; 14:28; 15:1; 17:1; 19:1; 21:1, 11, 13; 22:1; 23:1). The Hebrew word means "to lift up." The prophet was carrying a heavy weight because of the solemn nature of his message (Jer. 23:33). He was announcing judgments that involved the destruction of cities and the slaughter of thousands of people. No wonder he felt burdened!

*[handwritten: Gen 11:4 "a tower that reaches heaven"]*

## BABYLON (13:1—14:23; 21:1–10)

The word *Babel* means "gateway to a god" and sounds like the Hebrew word *balal*, which means "confusion" (Gen. 10:8–10; 11:1–9). In Scripture, Babylon symbolizes the world system man has built in defiance of God. Jerusalem and Babylon are contrasting cities: One is the chosen city of God, the other the wicked city of man. The city of God will last forever, but the rebellious city of man will ultimately be destroyed (Rev. 14:8; 16:19; 17–18).

*[handwritten margin: city of God / rebellious city]*

**God musters His army (13:1–5, 17–18).** God is sovereign. He is able to call any army He desires, to accomplish any task He assigns. He can summon them with a whistle (7:18) or by using leaders to raise a banner, shout, and beckon to the soldiers (13:2). In this case, God is mustering the army of the Medes (v. 17; 21:2), and He calls them "my sanctified ones." Even though they did not believe in Jehovah God, the Medes were set apart by God to do His holy work.

**God punishes His enemies (13:6–22).** The city of Babylon was completely destroyed in 689 BC by Sennacherib and the Assyrian army, but it was rebuilt by Sennacherib's son. In 539 BC, Darius the Mede captured the city (Dan. 5:31), but he did not destroy it. In the centuries that followed, Babylon had its "shining moments," but after the death of its last great conqueror, Alexander the Great, the city declined and soon was no more. Isaiah's prophecy was fulfilled, for the city was not rebuilt.

But it is clear that Isaiah's prophecy describes something more significant than the ups and downs of an ancient city. The prophets often began a message by focusing on local events, but then enlarged their vision to reveal something greater. Isaiah saw in the fall of Babylon a picture of "the day of the LORD" (Isa. 13:6, 9, 13), that time when God will pour out His wrath on the whole world (v. 11). The image of the woman in travail is used in Scripture to describe a time of judgment (v. 8; 21:3; 26:17; Jer. 6:24; Mic. 4:9–10; Matt. 24:8, where "sorrows" is "birthpains"; 1 Thess. 5:3). Isaiah looked beyond that day to the day when the Babylonian world system would be destroyed (Rev. 17—18). (Compare Isaiah 13:10 and Matthew 24:29; Joel 2:10; and Revelation 6:12–14; and see Jeremiah 50—51.)

**God delivers His people (14:1–23).** Isaiah warned that the kingdom of Judah would be taken into captivity by Babylon (5:13; 6:11–12; 11:11, where "Shinar" is Babylon; 39:6), and this happened in 586 BC. Jeremiah prophesied that the captivity would last for seventy years. Then Babylon would be judged and the Jews permitted to go home (Jer. 25:1–14). So, the capture of Babylon by Darius would be good news to the Jews; for it would mean the end of their exile and bondage.

The picture in Isaiah 14:1–23 is that of a mighty monarch whose pride has brought him to destruction. This is what happened to Belshazzar when Darius the Mede captured Babylon in 539 BC (Dan. 5). Isaiah described the king's arrival in sheol, the world of the dead, where the king's wealth, glory, and power vanished. The dead kings already in sheol stood in tribute to him (Isa. 14:9), but it was all a mockery. Death is the great leveler; there are no kings in the world of the dead. "Lucifer" (v. 12) is Latin for "morning star" and suggests that this king's glory did not last very long. The morning star shines but is soon swallowed up by the light of the sun.

The prophet saw in this event something far deeper than the defeat of

> Now is the time for the judgement of this world. now the prince of this world will be driven out."

← Satan masquerades as an angel of light

an empire. In the fall of the king of Babylon, he saw the defeat of Satan, the "prince of this world," who seeks to energize and motivate the leaders of nations (John 12:31; Eph. 2:1–3). Daniel 10:20 indicates that Satan has assigned "princes" (fallen angels) to the various nations so that he can influence leaders to act contrary to the will of God.

This highest of God's angels tried to usurp the throne of God and capture for himself the worship that belongs only to God (Matt. 4:8–10). The name "Lucifer" ("morning star") indicates that Satan tries to imitate Jesus Christ, who is "the bright and morning star" (Rev. 22:16). "I will be like the Most High" reveals his basic strategy, for he is an imitator (Isa. 14:14; 2 Cor. 11:13–15). Like the king of Babylon, Satan will one day be humiliated and defeated. He will be cast out of heaven (Rev. 12) and finally cast into hell (20:10). Whether God is dealing with kings or angels, Proverbs 16:18 is still true: "Pride goes before destruction, and a haughty spirit before a fall" (NKJV).

**God announces the victory (21:1–10).** "The desert of the sea" is probably the area around the Persian Gulf. Isaiah uses the image of a "desert storm" as he describes the attack of the Assyrians against Babylon, which took place in 689 BC. At that time, Babylon and Assyria were rival powers (although Assyria was stronger), and the nations in the Fertile Crescent hoped that Babylon would stop the advance of Assyria. Alas, Babylon fell to Assyria, opening the way for Assyria to sweep across the region in conquest.

Realizing the consequences of Babylon's fall, the prophet experienced pain like a woman in travail (vv. 3–4) and felt crushed like grain in a mill (v. 10). Had this announcement referred to the fall of Babylon in 539 BC, the Jews would have rejoiced; for it would have meant release from captivity. But in 689 BC, Babylon's defeat meant the destruction of the northern kingdom and the devastation of the southern kingdom. Note that Jeremiah (Jer. 51:8) and John (Rev. 14:8; 18:2) both adopted Isaiah's words, "Babylon is fallen, is fallen!"

*[handwritten: v27 For the Lord Almighty has purposed who can thwart him?]*

## ASSYRIA (14:24–27)

The key word here is *purpose*. God is in control of the rise and fall of the nations as He works out His divine purposes in the world. Assyria was His tool to accomplish His purposes (10:5), and the day would come when God would judge Assyria (see vv. 5ff.). *[handwritten: rod of my anger club of my wrath]*

The judgment would take place in the land of Judah, and God would be the judge. Assyria invaded Judah during Hezekiah's reign (701 BC), and God destroyed the army as it threatened to capture Jerusalem (37:36). God permitted Assyria to discipline Judah, but He would not allow the enemy to destroy His people.

## PHILISTIA (14:28–32)

An Assyrian leader ("rod"; 10:15, 24) died, and the Philistines rejoiced that their enemy had been weakened. (Some scholars think this leader was Shalmaneser V.) But Isaiah warned them that their rejoicing was presumptuous, for the new king would be worse. Isaiah compared the dead Assyrian ruler to a snake that gave birth to an even worse serpent! "Weep, Philistine cities—you are doomed" (14:31 TLB).

Note in this prophecy that God had a special word of assurance for His own people, Judah. Even the poorest of the poor would have food and safety (v. 30) and Zion would be delivered from the enemy (v. 32; 37:36), but the Philistines would be wiped out by war and famine (14:30). The Assyrian army would come from the north like a great cloud of smoke (v. 31), and the gates of the great Philistine cities would not stop them.

The envoys ("messengers" in v. 32) of the other nations would ask what was happening, but the diplomatic news would focus on Judah and not on Philistia! God's deliverance of Judah was the real news, not Assyria's conquest of Philistia. We wonder if diplomats and news reporters in today's media world would give God credit for a miracle of deliverance.

## MOAB (15:1—16:14)

The Moabites were the product of Lot's incestuous union with his daughter (Gen. 19:30–38) and were the avowed enemies of the Jews (Num. 25; 31; Deut. 23:3).

**The plight of Moab (15:1–9).** Within three years (16:14), this prophecy against Moab would be fulfilled with great national lamentation. At least fourteen different references to lamentation occur in this chapter: weeping, wailing, baldness, sackcloth, crying out, etc. The people fled to their temples and prayed to their gods, but to no avail (15:2 NIV). Even a day of national humiliation did not stop Assyria from invading Moab and ravaging the land. Advancing armies often stopped up the springs and watercourses and left the land in desolation (vv. 6–7). Where there was water in Moab, it was stained with blood, so great was the carnage (v. 9). How could the weak Moabites ever hope to defeat the great Assyrian lion?

**The plea of Moab (16:1–5).** The one place the Assyrians could not conquer was Jerusalem (10:24–34). Though the Assyrian army entered the kingdom of Judah and did a great deal of damage to the land, it could not capture Jerusalem (chaps. 36—37). However, instead of fleeing to Mount Zion, the Moabite fugitives fled south to the fords of the Arnon River and the "rock city" of Sela in Edom.

From Sela, the fugitives sent an appeal to the king of Judah to give them asylum from the enemy. But Isaiah warned them that it would take more than a request: They would need to submit to the king of Judah, which meant acknowledging the God of Judah. In that day, sending animals to a ruler was a form of paying tribute (2 Kings 3:4). Moab begged the leaders of Judah to give them refuge from the enemy, like a protecting rock on a hot day (16:3–4; see 32:1–2).

Isaiah was not impressed with the appeals of the Moabites. He called the Moabites extortioners, spoilers, and oppressors, and announced that the nation was destined to be destroyed (16:4). Why? Because they wanted

Judah's help, but they did not want Judah's God. Verse 5 is definitely a messianic promise, pointing to the day when the Messiah will reign in righteousness and mercy on David's throne. But Moab would not submit; they wanted deliverance on their own terms.

**The pride of Moab (16:6–14).** We can understand the pride of a city like Babylon (14:12–14), but what did the tiny nation of Moab have to boast about? Their pride kept them from submitting to Judah, and this led to their defeat. Their boasting would turn into wailing and their songs into funeral dirges. Moab would become like a vineyard trampled down and a fruitful field left unharvested. Isaiah 16:9–11 describes the prophet's grief—and the Lord's grief—over the destruction of Moab. "I have no pleasure in the death of the wicked" (Ezek. 33:11). Isaiah could have rejoiced at the destruction of an old enemy, but instead he wept (Prov. 24:17–18).

## DAMASCUS [SYRIA] AND EPHRAIM [ISRAEL] (17:1–14)

These two nations were allied in their opposition to both Assyria and Judah (7:1–2), so the prophet spoke to both in one message. In 17:1–2, he warned Damascus, the capital city of Aram (Syria), that the city would be taken by the enemy. This occurred when the Assyrians conquered Aram in 732 BC. Following their usual custom, the Assyrians deported many of the citizens, which left the land and cities deserted.

The fall of Damascus was a warning to Israel, the northern kingdom that had broken away from Judah and Judah's God (1 Kings 12). The prophet used several images to describe Ephraim's downfall: the destruction of the fortified cities (Isa. 17:3); the setting of the sun (v. 4a; "The glory has departed," 1 Sam. 4:19–22 NKJV); the wasting away of a sick person (Isa. 17:4b); the gleaning of a small harvest (vv. 5–6); the decaying of a garden into a wasteland (vv. 9–11); the overflowing of a flood (vv. 12–13a); and the blowing away of chaff and tumbleweeds in a storm (v. 13b).

When judgment came, the people of Israel realized that their idols could not save them; so they turned to the Lord for help, but it was too late (Prov. 1:20–33). The nation was sick with sin and beyond recovery. Once the wind began to blow and the floods began to rise, the nation was without hope. In 722 BC, Assyria conquered, and the kingdom of Israel was no more.

The emphasis in this section is on the God of Israel. He is the Lord of Hosts (the Lord almighty), who controls the armies of heaven and earth (Isa. 17:3). He is the Lord God of Israel (v. 6), who called and blessed Israel and warned her of her sins. He is our Maker, the Holy One of Israel (v. 7); He is the God of our salvation and our Rock (v. 10). How foolish of the Israelites to trust their man-made idols instead of trusting the living God (v. 8; 1 Kings 12:25–33). But like Israel of old, people today trust the gods they have made instead of the God who made them; these include the false gods of pleasure, wealth, military might, scientific achievement, and even "religious experience."

## ETHIOPIA (18:1–7)

The original text has "Cush," a land that covers the area now occupied by Ethiopia, the Sudan, and Somalia. Isaiah called it "a land of whirring wings" (v. 1 NIV), not only because of the insects that infested the land, but also because of the frantic diplomatic activity going on as the nation sought alliances to protect themselves from Assyria. He pictures the ambassadors in their light, swift boats, going to the African nations for help. But God tells them to go back home (v. 2) because He would deal with Assyria Himself, apart from the help of any army.

In contrast to the frantic human activity on earth is the calm patience of God in heaven (v. 4) as He awaits the right time to reap the harvest of judgment. Assyria is pictured as a ripening vine that will never survive, for God will cut it down (v. 5). In verse 6, Isaiah describes the feast that God spreads for the birds and beasts, the corpses of 185,000 Assyrian soldiers (37:36). (See Revelation 14:14–20; 19:17–21, where these same two images are used for end-time judgments.)

Instead of rushing here and there with diplomatic plans, the Cushites will go to Jerusalem with gifts for the Lord and for the king of Judah (Isa. 17; 2 Chron. 32:20–23). When the messianic kingdom is established, the Gentile nations will go to Mount Zion to worship the Lord and bring Him gifts (Isa. 60:1–7).

## EGYPT (19:1—20:6)

The late Dr. Wilbur M. Smith, a leading prophetic scholar, wrote that Isaiah 19 "contains the most important prophetic utterance concerning Egypt in all of the Old Testament" (*Egypt in Biblical Prophecy*, 77). It is a remarkable prophecy, for Isaiah declares that the three enemies—Egypt, Israel, and Assyria (modern Iraq)—will one day be united in worshipping the Lord and sharing His blessing!

**God will judge Egypt (19:1–15; 20:1–6).** This prophecy was probably fulfilled in 670 BC when Egypt was conquered by Esar-haddon, king of Assyria. The Assyrian conquest proved that the many gods of Egypt were powerless to help (19:1), and that the mediums and wizards were unable to give counsel (v. 3). In the days of Moses, God triumphed over the gods of Egypt (Ex. 12:12; Num. 33:4) and the wisdom of the Egyptian leaders, and He would do it again.

But that is not all. The forty-two provinces of Egypt, called "nomes," would be thrown into disarray and start fighting each other (Isa. 19:2). The Nile River, the source of Egypt's economy, and the streams and canals of the land, would all dry up; this would put farmers, fishermen, and cloth manufacturers out of business (vv. 5–10). For centuries, the Egyptians were respected for their wisdom, but now the princes and counselors would not know what to do (vv. 11–13). Instead of walking a straight path, the nation was led astray by leaders who were as dizzy as a drunken man staggering around in his vomit (vv. 14–15). Not a very pretty picture!

In these days of almost instant communication and of rapid transportation, when in a matter of minutes nations can come to the brink of war, we forget that God is still sovereign and can do whatever He pleases in the affairs of men. God destroyed everything that the Egyptians trusted—their political unity, their economy, religion, wisdom—and made them an easy target for the Assyrians. When the international news is frightening and you wonder where God is, read Psalm 2 and Acts 4:23–32, and take hope.

Isaiah 20 is a footnote to this prophecy and reveals that Isaiah did some unique things to get the attention of the people of Judah. One faction wanted to make an alliance with Egypt and Cush, but Isaiah warned them that such allies were destined to fall. For three years, the prophet dressed like a prisoner of war, wearing only a loincloth, to demonstrate his message. The pro-Egyptian party in Judah gave the prophet as much trouble as the pro-Egyptian people did who journeyed with Moses (30:1–7; 31:1–3; Num. 11; 14).

**God will save Egypt (19:16–25).** The phrase "in that day" is used five times in this passage and refers to the last days when Jesus Christ shall establish His messianic kingdom on earth. Some remarkable changes will take place. Egypt will fear Israel (vv. 16–17) and become converted to the worship of the true God (vv. 18–22). They will trust Him, not their idols, and pray to Him in times of need. This is a promise that vast numbers of Muslims in Egypt will one day turn to the Lord and be saved!

These spiritual changes will bring about a great political change: Israel, Egypt, and Assyria (modern Iraq) will cooperate and enjoy the blessing of the Lord! They will not only receive God's blessing, but they will all be a blessing to the other nations (vv. 23–25). Once again, Isaiah picks up his "highway" theme to emphasize the unity of these three nations (see 11:16). What a wonderful day it will be when there is peace in the Middle East because the nations have bowed before the King of Kings! We must continue praying, "Even so, come, Lord Jesus" (Rev. 22:20).

## EDOM (21:11–12)

Dumah and Seir are names for Edom (Num. 24:18). Isaiah moved one letter in the Hebrew word *Adom* and created *Dum*, which means "stillness, silence." It was his way of saying, "Edom will be silent; it will be no more." The Edomites were descendants of Esau, whose nickname was "red [Edom]" (Gen. 25:21–34). Edom was a rugged land of red sandstone; her people were bitterly hostile to the Jews (Ps. 137:7).

Isaiah was the watchman on the wall (Isa. 21:6; Ezek. 3:16–21; 33:1–11), and he was asked, "What of the night?" What time of night was it? The advance of the Assyrian army had brought fearful darkness to the nations, and Edom wanted to know if there was any hope, any light. The prophet's reply was brief but adequate, with both information and invitation. Morning was coming, because Assyria would be defeated by God in the fields of Judah (Isa. 37:36). But the morning would not last, for Babylon would take Assyria's place and bring further darkness to the nations.

Then Isaiah added an invitation consisting of three simple words: *inquire, return, come.* "Seek the Lord," urged the prophet. "Turn from sin and return to Him. Come to Him, and He will receive you!" A brief "day of salvation" would dawn, and they had better use the opportunity.

Edom did not heed the invitation. The nation was taken by Babylon, then by the Persians (who changed their name to "Idumea"), and finally by the Romans. The battle between Esau and Jacob was carried on by Herods, who were Idumeans. After the fall of Jerusalem in AD 70, Edom vanished from the scene.

## ARABIA (21:13–17)

The prophet saw the caravans of the Arabian merchants from Dedan leaving the trade route and hiding in the thickets because of the invasion of the Assyrian army. Food and water were brought to the fugitives by people from Tema, an oasis town. Eventually the caravan had to flee, for how could the merchants' slow animals compete with the Assyrian cavalry or their bows with the invaders' weapons? Like a laborer, God had a "contract" to fulfill (16:14). Within a year, the pomp and glory of the Arabian tribes would be gone.

## JUDAH AND JERUSALEM (22:1–25)

The people of Judah were behaving like their pagan neighbors, so it was only right that Isaiah should include them in the list of nations God would judge. Yes, in His mercy, the Lord would deliver Jerusalem from the Assyrian army, but He would not deliver them from Babylon. Isaiah pointed out two particular sins that would cause Judah to decline and ultimately go into captivity in Babylon.

(1) **The unbelief of the people (vv. 1–14).** While some parts of this description may seem to apply to the Assyrian invasion in Hezekiah's day (chaps. 36—37; 2 Kings 18—19; 2 Chron. 32), the primary reference is to the Babylonian conquest of Jerusalem in 586 BC. In Isaiah's day, Jerusalem was a "joyous city" as people engaged in all kinds of celebrations (Isa. 5:11–13; 32:12–13). The popular philosophy was, "Let us eat and drink; for tomorrow we shall die" (22:13; 56:12; 1 Cor. 15:32). But the prophet did not participate in the parties, for he saw a day coming when death and destruction would reign in the City of David. The people went up to the housetops, but the prophet went down into one of the three valleys around Jerusalem; there God gave him a vision. Visions and valleys often go together.

He saw people dying, not from battle wounds, but from famine and disease (Isa. 22:2). He saw the nation's rulers fleeing in fear as the enemy army approached (vv. 3–7; 2 Kings 25:1–10). The people would do every-thing possible to prepare for a long siege (Isa. 22:8–11): collecting armor (1 Kings 7:2; 10:17), fortifying the walls (Isa. 22:9–10), servicing the water supply (v. 9; 2 Chron. 32:1–4, 30; 2 Kings 20:20), and building a reservoir between the walls (Isa. 22:11). But all of this frantic preparation would not deliver them from the enemy. "The defenses of Judah are stripped away (v. 8 NIV). In their false confidence, they said, "Just as the Lord delivered Jerusalem from Assyria, so He will deliver us from Babylon."

The people did everything but trust the Lord (v. 11). Instead of feasting, they should have been fasting, weeping, putting on sackcloth, and pulling out their hair in grief (v. 12; Ezra 9:3; James 4:8–10). God had sent the nation many prophets to warn them, but the people would not listen. Now it was too late; their sins could not be forgiven because their hearts were hard. Judah would go into captivity, and God's word to Isaiah would be fulfilled (Isa. 6:9–13).

**(2) The unfaithfulness of the leaders (vv. 15–25).** Had the leaders been faithful to the Lord and called the people to repentance, there might have been hope, but too many of the leaders were like Shebna, thinking only of themselves. As treasurer (steward), Shebna was second to King Hezekiah in authority (see chaps. 36—37), but he used his authority (and possibly the king's money) to build himself a monumental tomb (22:16) and to acquire chariots (v. 18; see 2:7). Shebna was not a spiritual man, and he probably sided with the pro-Egypt party in Judah.

God judged Shebna by demoting him (he became "secretary" according to 36:3 NIV), disgracing him, and deporting him. Eventually he was thrown "like a ball" (22:18) into a far country (Assyria?), where he died. He could not have an expensive funeral and be buried in his elaborate tomb.

God chose a new man, Eliakim ("God will raise up"), and called him "my servant." Instead of exploiting the people, he would be a father to them and use his "key" (authority) for the good of the nation. He would be like a dependable peg, hammered into the wall, on which you could hang many burdens. But even a godly leader like Eliakim could not prevent the ultimate fall of Judah, for one day the whole nation would fall (v. 25). Eliakim is a picture of Jesus Christ (Rev. 3:7), the greatest Servant of all.

## PHOENICIA (23:1–18)

The Phoenicians were a merchant people whose land approximated what is today known as Lebanon. Their ships plied the Mediterranean coasts, where their many colonies assured them of an abundant supply of the world's wealth. Tyre and Sidon were key cities. Both David and Solomon made use of workers and building materials from Phoenicia (2 Sam. 5:11; 1 Kings 5:8–9). King Ahab married the Phoenician princess Jezebel, who promoted Baal worship in Israel (1 Kings 16:29–33).

**Declaration (vv. 1–7).** Isaiah addressed ships from Spain (Tarshish) that were docked at Cyprus (Kittim), telling their crews to weep and go home (v. 6) because Tyre was no more. Merchants from Spain, the coastlands, and even Egypt would wail because Tyre's great shipping industry was gone and the Mediterranean economy had been devastated. (See Rev. 17—18 for a parallel, and note that both Babylon and Tyre are compared to prostitutes [Isa. 23:16–17]). The joyful citizens of Tyre would become mourning refugees (v. 7) when Nebuchadnezzar would conquer Phoenicia in 572 BC. (He did not conquer the island part of Tyre, but Alexander the Great would do it in 332 BC. See Ezek. 26.)

**Explanation (vv. 8–14).** "Who planned this against Tyre?" (v. 8 NIV). The Lord Almighty! Just as He purposed to destroy Egypt (19:23) and Babylon (14:22), so He purposed to judge Tyre. Just as Assyria had destroyed the city of Babylon in 689 BC, so Tyre and Sidon would be destroyed by a revived Babylon in 585–572 BC (23:13). The pride of Tyre (v. 9) was a sin that God could not ignore.

**Anticipation (Isa. 23:15–18).** Even before their eventual destruction, Tyre and Sidon would not be involved in business for seventy years. History tells us that the Assyrians restricted Phoenician trade from 700–630 BC; but when Assyria began to weaken in power, Tyre and Sidon revived their businesses. The prophet compared the revived city to an old prostitute who had to sing lovely songs in order to get attention. Apparently the shipping business would not be as easy or as lucrative as it once was. In verse 18, Isaiah looked ahead to the messianic kingdom, when the wealth of Tyre would not be hoarded (see Zech. 9:3), but given to the Lord as a holy offering.

Our trek through these eleven chapters has taught us some important lessons. First, God is in control of the nations of the world, and He can do with them what He pleases. "Though the mills of God grind slowly, yet they grind exceeding small" (Friedrich von Logau, translated by Henry Wadsworth Longfellow). Second, God especially hates the sin of pride (see Isa. 13:11; 16:6; 23:9; Prov. 8:13). When nations turn from the living God to trust their wealth and their armaments, God must show them that He is the only sure refuge. Third, God judges the nations for the way they treat each other. Judah was the only nation mentioned that had God's law, yet God held the other ten Gentile nations accountable for what they did. "For as many as have sinned without law will also perish without law" (Rom. 2:12 NKJV). Finally, God always gives a word of promise and hope to His people. Babylon will fall, but God will care for Judah (Isa. 14:1–3, 32). Moab will not accept sanctuary from Jerusalem, but God will one day establish the Messiah's throne there (16:5). Assyria and Egypt may be avowed enemies of the Jews, but one day the three nations will together glorify God (19:23–25).

Therefore, no matter how frightening the national or international situation may become, God's children can have peace because they know Almighty God is on His throne. The nations may rage and plot against God, but "He who sits in the heavens shall laugh" (Ps. 2:4 NKJV).

When the Lord of heaven and earth is your Father, and you gladly wear Christ's yoke, you have nothing to fear (Matt. 11:25–30). Therefore, be comforted!

# QUESTIONS FOR PERSONAL REFLECTION
# OR GROUP DISCUSSION

1. From what you know of Scripture, what evidence is there that history is going somewhere, and that there is Someone in charge?

2. How does the geographical location of Israel/Palestine reveal God's sovereignty (see Ezek. 5:5)? Why do you think God placed Israel/Palestine in the center of the nations?

   *This is Jerusalem, which I have set in the center of the nations with countries all around her. Ez 5:5*

3. What advantages and disadvantages might there be for God's people—economically, politically, spiritually—being at the crossroads of civilization?

4. "Babylon symbolizes the world system man has built in defiance of God." What are some aspects of that world system today? How does God describe Babylon in Isaiah 13:1—14:23?

5. What does Isaiah prophesy will happen on the day of the Lord (Isa. 13)?

6. Isaiah 14:12–17 seems to look beyond the king of Babylon to Lucifer, the ruler of the defiant world system. How does this passage portray Lucifer (Satan)? How do you see him at work in the events of this world?

7. If God used Assyria as "a tool to accomplish His purposes," how could He then hold them accountable for that?

8. What gods do people worship in place of the one true God?

9. How can Psalm 2 and Acts 4:23–31 give you hope when the international news is not good?

10. Isaiah invited Edom to "inquire, return, come." What did this mean? What was that nation's response? In what area of your life might God be inviting you to do this?

# Chapter Five

# A Refuge from the Storm

## (Isaiah 24—27)

After prophesying concerning eleven different nations, Isaiah enlarged his prophecy and described a judgment that would fall on the whole world. The Hebrew word *erets,* used sixteen times in chapter 24, is translated "land," "earth," and "world" in the King James Version. It is not always easy to tell when *erets* refers to one country or to the whole earth, but the context usually guides us. Isaiah 24—27 describes a global judgment that will end with the destruction of God's enemies and the restoration of God's people, Israel, in their land.

Isaiah warned the northern kingdom that the Assyrians would destroy them, and he told Judah that the Babylonians would take them captive, but these local calamities were only forerunners of a vast end-times catastrophe that would engulf the whole world. The prophets call this time of terrible judgment "the day of the Lord," and in the New Testament it is described in Matthew 24, Mark 13, and Revelation 6—19.

Isaiah made three declarations that would comfort God's chosen people in that awesome day of judgment. These declarations also encourage us today as we see our world plunging headlong into sin and rebellion against God. Will God ever deal with the wicked? What hope is there for the righteous?

## 1. THE LORD WILL JUDGE HIS ENEMIES (24:1–23)

The result of God's judgment will be a world that is empty, laid waste, and distorted, and whose inhabitants are scattered. The prophet may have had Genesis 1:2 and 11:9 in mind when he wrote this. Nobody on earth will escape, for "God is no respecter of persons" (Acts 10:34). Position, power, and wealth are no protection against the wrath of God. God merely speaks the word and, like a dying invalid, "the world languishes and fades away" (Isa. 24:4 NKJV). People who are proud of their wealth and position will find themselves poor and without power.

Why does God punish the inhabitants of the world? Because they have defiled the world by their sins. When Adam sinned, God cursed the ground as a part of the punishment (Gen. 3:17–19; Rom. 8:20–22), and God warned the people of Israel that their sins polluted the Promised Land (Num. 35:33). Today we see man's greed polluting land, water, and atmosphere, as well as exploiting the earth of its God-given treasures. Sin has consequences in nature as well as in human character and conscience.

For centuries, mankind has polluted the world by disobeying God's laws and violating His statutes. This was the reason for the flood (Gen. 6:5, 11–13). Long before Moses gave the law, people knew that it was wrong to lie, steal, and kill (Rom. 1:18—2:16), but they did these evil things anyway. The "everlasting covenant" of Isaiah 24:5 refers to what we generally call the Noahic covenant (Gen. 8:20—9:17) and deals primarily with our care of God's world and our treatment of fellow humans. Isaiah 24:16 suggests that God will also judge the world because people are treacherous and do not keep their word. The people of the world have abused both the earth and its inhabitants, and they will pay for it.

Verses 6–13 give a vivid picture of what it will be like on the earth during the day of the Lord. In Israel, the harvest was generally a time for great joy; but there will be no joy because there will be no harvest. God's judgments will destroy the crops as well as the workers who would till the soil (see

Rev. 6:8; 9:15). "The city" is mentioned at least eight times in these chapters (Isa. 24:10, 12; 26:5; 27:10) and should be taken generically rather than as a reference to any one particular city. Whether people live in rural areas or in the cities, they will not escape God's wrath. Like a farmer harvesting the last olive or the last grape, God will do a thorough job of judging sinners (24:13). The only singing during His harvest will be done by the believing remnant who trust God and are delivered (vv. 14–16a). The doctrine of "the remnant" is an important part of Isaiah's message (1:9; 10:20–22; 11:11, 16; 14:22, 30); Isaiah's eldest son was named "a remnant shall return" (7:3).

The prophet changed the image in 24:17–18a when he described the futile attempts of frightened animals to avoid the hunters' traps. But apart from faith in the Lord, there will be no place of escape in that great day of judgment. No matter where sinners go, they will not be able to hide from the wrath of God (Rev. 6:15–17).

The opening of the windows of heaven (Isa. 24:18b) reminds us of the flood (Gen. 7:11). Jesus said that, before the "day of the Lord," society would be as it was in the days before the flood (Matt. 24:37–42). In that day, God will shake everything, and anything man has made will stagger like a drunk and collapse like a flimsy hut (Isa. 24:20; see 1:8). The weight of guilt will be too heavy for people to carry.

But the day of the Lord will affect not only the earth and its people but also Satan and his hosts. God will judge "the powers in the heavens above" as well as "the kings on the earth below" (24:21 NIV). These judgments will be part of the spiritual battle that has been waging for centuries between the Lord of Hosts and the armies of the Devil (Gen. 3:15; Luke 10:17–24; Eph. 6:10ff.; Rev. 12). Isaiah 24:22 parallels Revelation 20:1–3, an event that will take place just before the thousand-year reign of Jesus Christ (Isa. 24:23; Rev. 20:4–10). The word *visited* in Isaiah 24:22 (KJV) means "released" (cf. NIV margin). The climax of the "day of the Lord" will be "the LORD of hosts shall reign in Mount Zion" (v. 23).

## 2. THE LORD WILL PRESERVE HIS PEOPLE (25:1–12)

This chapter is a song of praise to the Lord from the believing remnant that He preserved during "the day of the Lord." In this song, three striking images stand out.

(1) **The ruined city (vv. 1–3).** We have met this image before (24:10, 12) and noted that "the city" is a generic term for all cities. Isaiah lived in an agricultural world of towns and villages, and the large cities (or city-states) were places of power and wealth. In times of war, the people fled to the walled cities for protection. But the great cities of the world will offer no protection when God pours His wrath on the nations (2:19; Rev. 16:19). The rebellious cities will be forced to acknowledge the greatness of God and give their homage to Him.

(2) **The refuge (vv. 4–5).** Isaiah paints two pictures: the buffeting of a storm and the beating down of a burning sun in the desert. Where can travelers go for refuge? They see a huge rock and find refuge in it. God is that Rock (Deut. 32:3–4, 30; 33:27; Ps. 46:1; 61:1–4), and He will be a refuge for His believing people during that terrible "day of the Lord." The victory shouts of the enemy will disappear the way heat vanishes when a cloud covers the sun.

God cares for His own in times of trial and judgment. He kept Noah and his family alive through the flood (Gen. 6—8) and guarded Israel when His judgments fell on Egypt (Ex. 8:22–23; 9:4, 6, 26; 10:23; 11:6–7; 12:13). He protected believing Rahab and her family when Jericho fell (Josh. 6:25) and preserved a faithful remnant when Judah was taken into Babylonian captivity (Ezra 9:8–9). Throughout the centuries, He has kept His church in spite of the attacks of Satan (Matt. 16:18) and will deliver His church from the wrath to come (1 Thess. 1:10; 5:9). When "the day of the Lord" comes to this godless world, God will see to it that the Jewish remnant will be preserved. "Hide yourselves for a little while until his wrath has passed by. See, the LORD is coming out of his dwelling to punish the people of the earth for their sins" (Isa. 26:20–21 NIV).

**(3) The feast (vv. 6–12).** For the Old Testament Jew, a feast was a picture of the kingdom age when Messiah would reign over Israel and all the nations of the world. Israel would enter into her glory, and the Gentiles would come to Zion to worship the Lord (2:1–5; 55:1–5; 60:1ff.). When Jesus used the image of the feast in Matthew 8:11 and Luke 13:28–29, the people knew He was speaking about the promised kingdom.

The food that we eat only sustains life, but at this feast death itself will be conquered. "On this mountain he will destroy the shroud that enfolds all peoples, the sheet that covers all nations; he will swallow up death forever. The Sovereign LORD will wipe away the tears from all faces" (Isa. 25:7–8 NIV). The funeral will turn into a wedding! Verse 8 was quoted by Paul in 1 Corinthians 15:54 and by the apostle John in Revelation 7:17 and 21:4.

The "covering" and "veil" in Isaiah 25:7 may also suggest the blindness of Israel and the nations to the true God and Savior (2 Cor. 3:12–18; 4:3–4). When the Lord Jesus Christ returns in power and great glory, Israel "shall look upon me whom they have pierced" (Zech. 12:10) and shall trust in Him for salvation. The veil shall be removed, and they will see their Messiah and their God. Then they will sing the song of Isaiah 25:9 as they enter into the great kingdom feast.

In contrast to the exaltation of Mount Zion is the humiliation of Moab (vv. 10–12). Isaiah probably selected Moab as an example of how God will humble all of Israel's enemies. The imagery here is quite graphic: The Moabites are compared to straw trampled so deeply into manure that the people have to swim through the manure to get out! (See the NIV.) While the Jews are enjoying a feast of good things, the Moabites are trying to escape from the excrement of the animals the Jews are devouring! Moab was always known for its pride (16:6ff.), but God will bring them low along with all the other nations that exalt themselves, exploit others, and refuse to submit to the Lord.

## 3. THE LORD WILL RESTORE THE NATION (26:1—27:13)

Israel is singing once more (24:14–16; 25:1ff.), and this time the emphasis is on righteousness and peace. There can be no true peace apart from righteousness (32:17), and there can be no righteousness apart from God's salvation in Jesus Christ (Rom. 3:21–31). It is at Calvary that "righteousness and peace have kissed each other" (Ps. 85:10). When Jesus Christ reigns on earth, the promise of Psalm 72:7 will be fulfilled: "In His days the righteous shall flourish, and abundance of peace, until the moon is no more" (NKJV). Jesus Christ is our true Melchizedek—King of Righteousness and King of Peace (Heb. 7:1–3).

The phrase "in that day" (Isa. 26:1; 27:1–2, 12–13) refers to "the day of the Lord" and the blessings that will follow when the Lord defeats His enemies. In these two chapters, the prophet encourages God's suffering people by describing in seven pictures the kingdom blessings that await them in the future.

**(1) The strong city (26:1–6).** Samaria fell to the Assyrians and Jerusalem to the Babylonians, but the New Jerusalem would be impregnable. During "the day of the Lord," God will level the lofty cities of the earth, but Mount Zion will be exalted to the glory of the Lord (2:1–5). Jerusalem will no longer be the sinful city described in chapter 1; it will be a righteous city for a holy nation whose sins have been washed away (Zech. 13:1). Compare Isaiah 26:2 with Psalms 15 and 24.

Only those who have trusted Jesus Christ will enter into the city, and because they believe, they have peace (Rom. 5:1). The Hebrew word for peace *(shalom)* means much more than a cessation of war. It includes blessings such as wholeness, health, quietness of soul, preservation, and completeness. "What is your peace?" is the way Jews often greet one another, and Isaiah's reply would be "My peace is from the Lord, for I trust wholly in him!" Paul's counsel in Philippians 4:6–9 is based on Isaiah 26:3.

It is worth noting that Augustus Toplady's song "Rock of Ages" is based on the marginal reading of verse 4: "for in the Lord God is the Rock of ages." The New Jerusalem is a city built on a Rock!

**(2) The level path (26:7–11).** We have noted Isaiah's emphasis on the image of the highway (see comments at 11:16). During much of their history, the Jews have traveled a rough road, but when the kingdom is established, God will give them level paths and a smooth way. Because they will be walking in the will of God, their way will be safe and enjoyable. They will wait on the Lord to discern His will. They will yearn for the Lord and worship Him even in the night (Ps. 119:55).

According to Isaiah 26:9–11, God wants the world to learn righteousness. He sends His judgments, but the people still will not repent (Rev. 9:20–21; 16:9). He shows them His grace in a thousand ways, but they continue to do evil. His hand is at work, but they will not see it. The prophet prays that God will reveal Himself through His people as He works on their behalf. The reviving and restoring of Israel should help to convince a lost world that God is not dead and that He keeps His promises.

**(3) The woman in travail (26:12–18).** The agony of "the day of the Lord" is compared to the pain of a woman travailing in birth (13:6–8; 1 Thess. 5:1–3). Isaiah described the remnant confessing their failures to the Lord. Because of their sins, they had been subjected to many Gentile tyrants, but now these tyrants were dead and could not return to enslave them. God disciplined His people and brought them to the place where all they could do was whisper their prayers (Isa. 26:16 NIV), but He heard them and delivered them. Israel was in pain like a woman giving birth, except that their travail produced nothing! Israel failed to give birth to the blessings God wanted them to bring to the world (v. 18). But during the kingdom age, Israel and Mount Zion will be the source of blessing for the whole world.

What hindered Israel from being the blessing to the world that God wanted them to be? They turned from the sincere worship of the true

God and gave their devotion to idols. The Hebrew verb in verse 13 translated "had dominion" gives us the noun *baal,* the name of the Canaanite storm god whose cult created so many problems in Israel. But the word *baal* also means "husband," so the suggestion is that Israel was not true to her husband Jehovah, but in her unfaithfulness turned to another god. The same image occurs in James 4:4.

(4) **The life-giving dew (26:19–21).** Just as the dew brings new life to the soil and vegetation, so God will raise the dead out of the earth. The prophet had already announced God's great victory over death (25:7–8), and now he tells us how He will do it: He will raise their bodies from the dust. Resurrection is not reconstruction; God does not reassemble the body and give it life. Paul compared the miracle of resurrection to the harvesting of grain planted in the soil (1 Cor. 15:35–49). The seed is buried and dies, but out of this death comes forth life and fruitfulness. Isaiah had just written about travail (Isa. 26:17–18), so he compared the resurrection to human birth: "The earth will give birth to her dead" (v. 19 NIV).

When Christ returns for His church, believers who "sleep in Jesus" will be raised from the dead (1 Thess. 4:13–18). When He returns with His church to judge His enemies and establish His kingdom, there will also be a resurrection (Rev. 19:11—20:6). These two events are called "the first resurrection" and include only saved people. At the end of the thousand years, when Satan is finally imprisoned, the lost will be raised to face the Great White Throne Judgment (vv. 7–15). While the Old Testament does not give the complete revelation about death and resurrection, it does assure us that there is a future for the human body (Dan. 12:2; Ps. 16:9–10).

The remnant has been praying to God (Isa. 26:11–19), and now God speaks to them and gives them the assurance they need (vv. 20–21). He promises to shelter His people from the terrible attacks of the enemy (Rev. 12). God will punish His enemies who have slain His people, whose blood cries out from the earth for vengeance (Gen. 4:10–11; Ezek. 24:7–8; Rev.

6:9–11). The unjust shedding of blood pollutes the land (Num. 35:29–34; Ps. 106:34–39) and invites the judgment of God.

**(5) The conquered beast (27:1).** The nations around Israel had many myths about sea monsters, one of which was compared to "leviathan," probably the crocodile (Job 3:8; 41:1ff.). To slay leviathan was a great achievement (Ps. 74:14), and the Lord promised to do it. Satan held these nations in bondage through their superstitious religions, but the remnant did not need to fear the false gods of the Gentiles. God's people today are set free from bondage to Satan and the false gods he seduces people to worship (Col. 2:13–15), and we can rejoice in our Lord's great victory (John 12:31). When the battle is over and the Lord has conquered evil, Israel can enter her glorious kingdom without fear.

**(6) The fruitful vineyard (27:2–11).** As in 5:1–7, the vineyard is Israel, but here the prophet saw both the Israel of his day and the Israel of the future day when the kingdom will be established. God was not angry with His people (27:4); He just yearned for them to return to Him and fervently trust Him. He used war (Assyria) to punish the northern kingdom and captivity (Babylon) to discipline the southern kingdom (v. 8 NIV), but He did this in love and not in anger. Verses 10–11 are a description of Jerusalem after the Babylonian siege. God temporarily took away His mercy until His purposes were fulfilled.

In "the day of the Lord" God will use suffering to purge His people and prepare them for their kingdom. Verse 9 does not suggest that personal suffering can atone for sin, for only the sacrifice of Jesus Christ can do that. God uses suffering as a discipline to bring us to submission so that we will seek Him and His holiness (Heb. 12:1–11). The Babylonian captivity cured the Jews of their idolatry once and for all (Isa. 27:9).

In Isaiah's day, the vineyard was producing wild grapes, but in the future kingdom, Israel will be fruitful and flourishing. God will guard His people and give them all that they need to bring glory to His name. The nation will "blossom and bud, and fill the face of the world with fruit" (v. 6). Through Israel, all the nations of the earth will be blessed (Gen. 12:1–3).

The Bible speaks of three vines: the people of Israel (Isa. 5; 27); Christ and His church (John 15); and godless Gentile society, "the vine of the earth" (Rev. 14:18). The vineyard of Israel is not bearing fruit, the "vine of the earth" is filling the world with poisonous fruit, and God's people must be faithful branches in the Vine and produce fruit that glorifies God's name.

(7) **The holy and happy feast (27:12–13).** The camp of Israel was directed by the blowing of trumpets (Num. 10). The Feast of Trumpets took place on the first day of the seventh month and prepared Israel for the annual Day of Atonement (Lev. 23:23–32). But the Day of Atonement prepared them for the Feast of Tabernacles, which is a picture of the joy of the future kingdom (Lev. 23:33–44).

Isaiah envisioned a glorious day when God would repeat the miracle of the exodus and deliver His people from their bondage to the Gentile nations. The trumpet would summon them to Jerusalem (Matt. 24:31) and announce God's victory over their foes, and they would "worship the Lord in the holy mount at Jerusalem." The kingdom will be like an endless feast and a holy day of worship as the people rejoice in the Lord. Of course, God's people today are also awaiting "the sound of the trumpet" (1 Cor. 15:50–58; 1 Thess. 4:13–18) announcing the coming of the Lord for His church. Then we will go with Him to heaven and prepare for the marriage supper of Lamb. We shall return with Him to earth and reign with Him in the kingdom.

Are you praying daily, "Thy kingdom come"?

# QUESTIONS FOR PERSONAL REFLECTION
# OR GROUP DISCUSSION

1. What contemporary people can you think of who are models of repentance?

2. What condition will the earth be in at and after the day of the Lord? How will Satan, as well as the earth's inhabitants, be affected?

3. What environmental concerns of our day are the result of man's failure to be good stewards of the Lord's earth? How does Isaiah 24 speak to this situation?

4. Where can God's people go as they encounter life's storms? Describe a time when you experienced God as your refuge.

5. How did God care for His people during other times of trial and judgment (see Gen. 6—8; Ex. 8:22–23; Josh. 6:25; Ezra 9:8–9; Matt. 16:18)?

6. When you read about God's wrath and judgment, how do you respond? Why? What perspective does 1 Thessalonians 1:10 and 5:9 offer?

7. What significance is there in the feast (Isa. 25:6–9) that would give Christians hope?

8. What can we learn from Isaiah 26 about dealing with life's storms?

9. According to Hebrews 12:1–11, how does God use suffering as a discipline to purify us? How, if ever, have you experienced that?

10. Which of the kingdom blessings in Isaiah 26—27 seems especially important to you, and why?

11. How does this section of Isaiah flesh out what it means to pray, "thy kingdom come"?

# Chapter Six

# STORM CLOUDS OVER JERUSALEM

(Isaiah 28—31)

The name *Jerusalem* means "city of peace," but throughout its history it has been associated more with conflict than with peace. Even today, Jerusalem is a focal point for concern in the Middle East. "Pray for the peace of Jerusalem," admonished the psalmist (Ps. 122:6). Why pray for Jerusalem? Why not pray for London or Moscow or Rome? Because when there is true peace in Jerusalem, there will be peace in the whole world (Isa. 52:7; 66:12); so we had better take the psalmist's words to heart.

Chapters 28—31 record a series of five "woes" (28:1; 29:1, 15; 30:1; 31:1) that focus primarily on Jerusalem. A sixth "woe" is found in 33:1, and interspersed with these "woes" of judgment are promises of restoration and glory. Isaiah is attempting to get the rulers of Judah to stop trusting "power politics" and international treaties and start trusting the Lord.

## 1. THE LORD WARNS JERUSALEM (28:1–29)

Like all devout Jews, Isaiah loved Jerusalem, the Holy City, the City of David, the place of God's dwelling (Ps. 122; 137). But Isaiah saw storm clouds gathering over the city and announced that trouble was coming. It was time for the nation to turn to God in repentance.

He began his message by announcing God's judgment on Ephraim (Isa. 28:1–6). Surely their neighbor's fall would serve as a warning to the people of Judah and Jerusalem! If Assyria conquered Samaria, then Judah was next on the list. The northern kingdom was proud of its capital city, Samaria, that sat like a beautiful crown (or wreath) at the head of a fruitful valley. But their arrogance was detestable to God, for they thought their fortress city was impregnable. Samaria reigned in luxury and pleasure and had no fear of her enemies.

The Lord was also appalled by their drunkenness. To the Jews, wine was a gift from God and a source of joy (Judg. 9:13; Ps. 104:15). The law did not demand total abstinence, but it did warn against drunkenness (Deut. 21:18–21; Prov. 20:1; 23:20–21, 29–35). The prophet Amos denounced the luxurious indulgences of the people in both Judah and Samaria (Amos 6:1–7), and Isaiah also thundered against such godless living (Isa. 5:11–12, 22).

A government official in Washington, D.C., once quipped, "We have three parties in this city: the Democratic Party, the Republican Party, and the cocktail party." Indeed, Washington, D.C., ranks high on the list of cities noted for alcohol consumption. Many people don't realize that alcohol and nicotine, America's favorite legal narcotics, do far more lethal damage than all the illegal drugs combined. According to Dr. Arnold Washton, alcohol and nicotine kill more people annually than illegal drugs (*Willpower's Not Enough*, Harper & Row, 1989; 13). This does not make illegal drugs acceptable, but it does help us put things in perspective. What hope is there for our affluent, pleasure-loving society that gives lip service to religion and ignores the tragic consequences of sin and the judgment that is sure to come?

Samaria was proud of her beauty, but that beauty was fading like a cut flower (28:1, 4) that could never stand before the coming tempest. God was sending a storm across the land, and their proud city would be destroyed by wind, rain, hail, and flood—the Assyrian army! Conquering Samaria would be as easy as plucking a fig from a tree! On that day of judgment, Samaria would learn too late that Jehovah, not Samaria, is the "crown of glory" and "diadem of beauty" (v. 5) and that He is a God of justice (vv. 5–6). The reference here is to God's deliverance of Jerusalem from Assyria, even when the enemy was at the very gates (chaps. 36—37).

Perhaps the people of Judah rejoiced to hear Isaiah announce the fall of their rival kingdom, but their celebration was short-lived; for the prophet announced that Judah was guilty of the same sins as Samaria and therefore was in danger of judgment (28:5–8). The priests and the prophets, who should have been examples to the people, were staggering drunk around the city and carousing at tables covered with vomit. Their counsel to the people did not come from the Spirit of God but from their own drunken delusions (see Eph. 5:18). They not only swallowed wine, but were "swallowed up on wine" (Isa. 28:7). This reminds us of the Japanese proverb: "First the man takes a drink, then the drink takes a drink, and then the drink takes the man."

But pride and drunkenness were not Judah's only sins; they also mocked God's prophet and rejected God's Word (vv. 9–13). Verses 9–10 are the words of the drunken prophets and priests as they ridiculed Isaiah. "He talks to us as though we were little children," they said. "He keeps saying the same things over and over again and uses the vocabulary of a child. There is certainly no need to take anything he says seriously!"

Society today often takes a similar attitude toward God's servants and God's Word. People are so intoxicated by intellectual pride that they laugh at the simple message of the gospel presented by humble witnesses (1 Cor. 1:18–31). The prophet Amos was ejected from the king's chapel because he was a simple farmer and not a member of the religious elite (Amos 7:10–17). Evangelist D. L. Moody was often laughed at because his speech was not polished, but God used him to bring many thousands to the Savior.

What was Isaiah's answer to this supercritical crowd of religious drunks? "If you will not listen to my simple speech in your own language,

God will speak to you with a language you do not understand. He will send the army of Assyria, whose language is foreign to you." This happened to both Ephraim and Judah. The Assyrians completely destroyed the southern kingdom in 722 BC; and in 701 BC, after devastating the land of Judah, they came to the very gates of Jerusalem.

This leads to Isaiah's third announcement: God offers His people rest (Isa. 7:4; 8:6–8), but they will not obey (hear) His Word (28:12–20). The prophet had given them a plain message that everybody could understand, but they rejected it. Their faith was in their political alliances and not in God (vv. 15, 18). In the days of King Ahaz, they made a secret treaty with Assyria, and in the days of King Hezekiah, they turned to Egypt for help (30:1–5; 31:1). But these "covenants with death and the grave" were destined to fail because God was not in them. The enemy would come like a flood, a storm, a whip (scourge), and there would be no escape. Ephraim would be destroyed, and Judah would be saved by the skin of her teeth. The bed they had made (their alliances) could not give them rest (see 28:12), and the covering they made (their treaties) would not cover them (see 31:1).

Their only hope was in the tried and true foundation stone (28:16), the "Rock of ages" (26:4; 8:14; 17:10). This is definitely a reference to the Messiah and is so interpreted in the New Testament (1 Peter 2:4–7; Rom. 9:33; Mark 12:10; see Ps. 118:22). If they had faith in Jehovah, they would not be rushing here and there, trying to forge alliances, a practice that only leads to shame and failure (Rom. 10:11). A solid rock is better protection than a flimsy covering of lies!

Isaiah's final announcement was that their confidence that God would not judge them was a delusion (Isa. 28:21–29). "But God defended His people in the past!" they argued. "What about David's victory over the Philistines at Mount Perazim [2 Sam. 5:17–21], or Joshua's victory over the Amorites at Gibeon [Josh. 10]?" But Joshua and David were godly leaders who trusted Jehovah and obeyed His Word. What Isaiah's scoffing opponents did not realize was that God would do a "strange work": He would use the enemy to fight against His own people! Just as a farmer has different tasks to perform and must adapt himself to each task, whether plowing or threshing, so God must do the work that is necessary to bring about His eternal purposes. He knows just what tool to use and when to use it.

Jerusalem watched the northern kingdom fall to the Assyrians, but this judgment did not bring them to repentance. When we start saying to ourselves, "It can never happen to me!"—it is sure to happen!

## 2. THE LORD HUMBLES JERUSALEM (29:1–14)

*Ariel* is a code name for Jerusalem and means "lion of God." The lion was a symbol of Assyria, so the prophet may have been saying, "Assyria is now God's lion, and Jerusalem is God's lion in name only." But the Hebrew word also means "an altar hearth," where the burnt offerings were sacrificed (Ezek. 43:13–18). "It [Jerusalem] shall be unto me as Ariel [an altar hearth]" (Isa. 29:2). In other words, it would become a place of slaughter.

God was going to humble the proud city. Instead of roaring and frightening the enemy, the lion would only whisper from the dust (v. 4). Instead of their sacrifices being accepted by God (v.1), the entire city would become an altar, and God would make His people a sacrifice.

When did these things happen? God began to "turn up the heat" in 701 BC when Assyria marched triumphantly through Judah and almost took Jerusalem. God defeated Assyria in an instant (37:36), "suddenly" (29:5), like blowing away dust or chaff (v. 6). This discipline should have brought Judah back to the Lord, but after the death of Hezekiah, they returned to their sins. So in 586 BC God sent the Babylonians, who conquered Jerusalem and destroyed it, taking thousands of Jews into captivity. God did His "strange work" and permitted His own people to be slain by the enemy. The city indeed was like an altar hearth, and thousands were sacrificed to the wrath of the enemy.

But Isaiah looked far down the highway of history to the end times when Jerusalem would be attacked by the armies of the world (vv. 7–8; Zech. 14:1–3). This is what prophetic students call "the battle of Armageddon," though that title is not used in Scripture (Rev. 14:14–20; 16:13–21). When it looks as though the city is about to fall, and the enemy armies are sure of victory, Jesus Christ will return and deliver His people (19:11–21). The enemy victory will vanish.

Why were the people of Jerusalem so ignorant of what was going on? Their hearts were far from God (Isa. 29:13). They went through the outward forms of worship and faithfully kept the annual feasts (v. 1; 1:10ff.), but it was not a true worship of God (Matt. 15:1–9). Going to the temple was the popular thing to do, but most of the people did not take their worship seriously. Therefore, God sent a "spiritual blindness" and stupor on His people so that they could not understand their own law. Such blindness persists today (Rom. 11:8; 2 Cor. 3:13–18). If people will not accept the truth, then they must become more and more blind and accept lies. (See John 9:39–41; 2 Thess. 2:1–12.)

## 3. THE LORD APPEALS TO JERUSALEM (29:15–24)

This "woe" exposed the devious political tactics of the rulers of Judah, who thought that God would not hold them accountable for what they were doing. They were trying to turn things upside down, the clay telling the potter what to do (see 45:9; 64:8; Jer. 18; Rom. 9:20). If only people would seek the counsel of the Lord instead of depending on their own wisdom and the fragile promises of men!

In Isaiah 29:17–24, Isaiah asked the people to look ahead and consider what God had planned for them. In their political strategy, they had turned things upside down, but God would one day turn everything around by establishing His glorious kingdom on earth. The devastated land would become a paradise, the disabled would be healed, and the outcasts would be enriched and rejoice in the Lord. There would be no more scoffers or ruthless people practicing injustice in the courts. The founders of the nation, Abraham and Jacob, would see their many descendants all glorifying the Lord.

In light of this glorious future, why should Judah turn to feeble nations like Egypt for help? God is on their side, and they can trust Him! Abraham went to Egypt for help and got into trouble (Gen. 12:10–20), and Isaac started for Egypt but was stopped by God (26:1–6). God cared for Jacob during all of his years of trial, and surely He could care for Jacob's children. It is tragic when a nation forgets its great spiritual heritage and turns from trusting the Lord to trusting the plans and promises of men.

At the Constitutional Convention in Philadelphia in 1787, Benjamin Franklin said, "I have lived, Sir, a long time, and the longer I live, the more convincing proofs I see of this truth—that God governs in the affairs of men. I therefore beg leave to move that henceforth prayers imploring the assistance of heaven and its blessings on our deliberations be held in this Assembly every morning."

Isaiah sought that attitude in Jerusalem; but instead he found only scoffing and unbelief.

## 4. THE LORD REBUKES JERUSALEM (30:1–33)

This fourth "woe" begins with God's rebuke of the nation's rebellion (vv. 1–17). Isaiah opened his prophecy with this accusation (1:2, 20, 23), and he ended it on that same note (63:10; 65:2). After all that God had done for His people, they turned away from Him and sought the help of feeble Egypt. Unlike the leaders of old—Moses (Num. 27:21), Joshua (Josh. 9:14), David (1 Sam. 30:7–8), and Jehoshaphat (1 Kings 22:7ff.)—the rulers of Jerusalem did not seek the will of God. Egypt was but a shadow, and what could a shadow do against the great Assyrian army?

Isaiah then uttered an oracle (burden) concerning the caravan that was then traveling from Jerusalem to Egypt with treasures to buy protection against Assyria (Isa. 30:6–7). He saw the burdened animals making their way through the difficult and dangerous terrain of the Negev (the south), and he cried, "It is all to no profit! It is useless! The Egyptians will help in vain!" In verse 7, which should be read in a recent translation, Isaiah gives a nickname to Egypt: "Rahab-hem-shebeth," which means "Rahab the do-nothing." (Rahab is one of the names for Egypt in the Old Testament.)

It was bad enough that Judah rebelled against God by trusting Egypt instead of trusting Jehovah, and depending on money instead of on God's power, but they even went so far as to completely reject the Word of God (vv. 8–11). God told Isaiah to make a placard that said, "This is a rebellious people, lying children, children that will not hear the law of the LORD" (v. 9). He carried this sign as he walked around Jerusalem, and no doubt most of the people laughed at him. The leaders did not want to hear God's truth; they wanted "pleasant words" from the false prophets, sermons that would not disturb their comfortable way of life. Is this situation much different today? (See Jer. 6:14; 8:11; 1 Kings 22:1–28.)

Decisions have consequences, and Isaiah told the people what would happen to Judah and Jerusalem because they were trusting their lies: Their wall of protection would suddenly collapse, shattered to pieces like a clay vessel (Isa. 30:12–14). When Assyria invaded the land, Egypt lived up to her nickname and did nothing. It was not till the last minute that God stepped in and rescued His people, and He did it only because of His covenant with David (37:35–36). During Assyria's invasion of Judah, the Jews were not able to flee on their horses imported from Egypt (30:16–17; Deut. 17:16), and one enemy soldier was able to frighten off a thousand Jews! What humiliation (see Deut. 32:30)!

Their only hope was to repent, return to the Lord, and by faith rest only in Him (Isa. 30:15; 8:6–7; 26:3; 28:12), but they would not listen and obey.

The prophet then turned from the subject of rebellion to the subject of restoration (30:18–26). "Yet the LORD longs to be gracious to you," he told the people; "he rises to show you compassion" (v. 18 NIV). God's grace is His favor toward those who do not deserve it, and it is only because of His grace that we have any blessings at all. Isaiah described that future day when Israel would be restored to her land to enjoy the blessings of the kingdom. They would be like liberated prisoners of war (v. 19). Instead of scoffing, they would listen to God's Word and put away their foolish idols. The land would be restored and become prosperous again, and God would bind up the bruises and heal the wounds of His people (v. 26; see 1:5–6). The "great slaughter" of verse 25 is the battle of Armageddon, which will occur just before the return of the Lord to deliver His people and establish His kingdom (Rev. 19:11–21).

His final theme in this "woe" is retribution (Isa. 30:27–33), the announcement that God will defeat the Assyrians. God used Assyria to discipline Judah, but He would not permit the Assyrians to take the city of David. Isaiah used several images to describe God's judgment of Assyria: a storm of fire and hail, a flood, the sifting of grain (see Amos 9:9), and the harnessing of a horse so that the enemy is led off like a farm animal.

Just as sheol was prepared for the king of Babylon (Isa. 14:9ff.), so Topheth was prepared for the king of Assyria. Topheth was a site outside Jerusalem where the worshippers of Molech sacrificed their children (2 Kings 16:3; 21:6; Jer. 7:31–32; 19:6, 11–14). It was defiled by Josiah (2 Kings 23:10), turned into a garbage dump, and named "Gehenna," which comes from *ge-ben-hinnom*, meaning "valley of the son of Himmon." That was the location of Topheth. "Gehenna" is the New Testament word for "hell." The funeral pyre for the great king of Assyria would be a garbage dump! How humiliating!

The Jews would rejoice greatly at the defeat of Assyria, not unlike their rejoicing at Passover to commemorate the defeat of Egypt. When the Jews celebrate Passover, they still have "a song in the night" (Matt. 26:30), and the "timbrels and harps" (Isa. 30:32) remind us of the songs of Miriam and the Jewish women at the Red Sea (Ex. 15:20–21).

## 5. THE LORD DEFENDS JERUSALEM (31:1–9)

This fifth "woe" is a brief summary of what Isaiah had already told the people. Indeed, he was teaching them "line upon line; here a little, and there a little" (28:10), and yet they were not getting the message.

Their faith was in men, not in God. They trusted in the legs of horses and the wheels of chariots, not in the hand of the Lord. God warned the Jewish kings not to go to Egypt for horses and chariots (Deut. 17:14–16), but Solomon ignored this warning (1 Kings 10:28–29). Going to Egypt for help had always been a temptation to the Jews (Ex. 13:17; 14:11–12; Num. 11:5, 18; 14:3ff.).

Why should the Lord fear the Assyrians? Does a lion fear a flock of sheep and their shepherds? Do the eagles fear as they hover over their young in the nest? God will pounce on Assyria like a lion and swoop down like an eagle, and that will be the end! In one night, the Assyrian army was wiped out (Isa. 37:36).

Think of the money Judah would have saved and the distress they would have avoided had they only rested in the Lord their God and obeyed His will. All their political negotiations were futile and their treaties worthless. They trusted the words of the Egyptians but not the Word of God!

As God's church today faces enemies and challenges, it is always a temptation to turn to the world or the flesh for help. But our first response must be to examine our hearts to see if there is something we need to confess and make right. Then we just turn to the Lord in faith and obedience and surrender to His will alone. We must trust Him to protect us and fight for us.

A friend of mine kept a card in his office desk that read, "Faith is living without scheming." In one statement, that is what Isaiah was saying to Judah and Jerusalem, and that is what he is saying to us today.

# QUESTIONS FOR PERSONAL REFLECTION OR GROUP DISCUSSION

1. What evidence can be found in Isaiah 28—31 of God's burdens or concerns for His people?

2. What examples or analogies does God use to get His people's attention and motivate them to change?

3. What are the consequences of failure to heed God's warnings?

4. What basis do God's people have for any future hope in their relationship with Him?

5. As for Jerusalem, what was her bottom-line problem (see Isa. 30:8–11; 1:31)?

6. What names and incidents in Scripture do you recall of God's people using illegitimate ways to accomplish His will?

7. Had Jerusalem obeyed God's will, what stresses might she have avoided?

8. When in your journey of faith have you been tempted to walk by sight and not by faith?

9. How does your nation, your church, or your family face temptations to trust in other things than God or compromise His will?

10. What are some principles to apply when faced with the temptation to compromise God's will and God's ways (see Prov. 3:5–6; Ps. 27:13–14; Ps. 139:23–24; Isa. 40:27–31; Phil. 4:6–7)?

# Chapter Seven

# FUTURE SHOCK AND FUTURE GLORY

## (Isaiah 32—35)

In 1919, American writer Lincoln Steffens visited the Soviet Union to see what the Communist Revolution was accomplishing. In a letter to a friend, he wrote, "I have seen the future, and it works." If he were alive today, he would probably be less optimistic, but in those days, "the Russian experiment" seemed to be dramatically successful.

A university professor posted a sign on his study wall that read, "The future is not what it used to be." Since the advent of atomic energy, many people wonder if there is any future at all. Albert Einstein said that he never thought about the future because it came soon enough!

In the four chapters that conclude the first section of his prophecy, Isaiah invites us to look at four future events to see what God has planned for His people and His world. These chapters are not human speculation; they are divinely inspired revelation, and they can be trusted.

## 1. A KING WILL REIGN (32:1–20)

At the beginning of its history, the nation of Israel was a theocracy, with God as King; it was not a monarchy led by human rulers. In the days of Samuel, the people asked for a king, and God gave them Saul (1 Sam. 8;

see Deut. 17:14–20). God did not establish a dynasty through Saul because Saul did not come from the tribe of Judah (Gen. 49:10). It was David who established both the dynasty for Israel's throne and the ancestry for Israel's Messiah (2 Sam. 7). Every devout Jew knew that the future Messiah-King would be the Son of David (Matt. 22:41–46).

In Isaiah 32:1, Isaiah wrote about "a king," but in 33:17, he called him "the king." By the time you get to verse 22, He is "our king." It is not enough to say that Jesus Christ is "a King" or even "the King." We must confess our faith in Him and say with assurance that He is "our King." Like Nathanael, we must say, "Rabbi, You are the Son of God! You are the King of Israel!" (John 1:49 NKJV).

In contrast to the evil rulers of Isaiah's day (Isa. 1:21–23), the Messiah will reign in righteousness and justice (32:1, 16; 33:5; see 9:7; 11:1–5). In addition, the King will be like a rock of refuge for the people (8:14; 17:10; 26:4; 28:16) and like a refreshing river in the desert (8:5–8; 33:21; 41:18; 48:18; 66:12). "He who rules over men must be just," said David, "ruling in the fear of God" (2 Sam. 23:3 NKJV).

Isaiah 32:3–4 describes the wonderful transformations that will occur because of Messiah's reign. Isaiah ministered to spiritually blind, deaf, and ignorant people (6:9–10; 29:10–12), but in the kingdom, all will see and hear God's truth as well as understand and obey it. (See 29:18; 42:7.) This will happen because the nation will have a new heart and enter into a new covenant with the Lord (Jer. 31:31–34).

The "churl" (Isa. 32:5–8) is the knave or scoundrel who uses his or her position for personal profit and not for the good of the people. In Isaiah's day, as in our own day, the common people admired "the rich and famous," even though the character and conduct of these "celebrities" deserved no respect. They had money, fame, and influence; and in the eyes of the populace, that made them important. But in the kingdom, there will be no such deception. "Wealthy cheaters will not be spoken of as generous, outstanding men! Everyone will recognize an evil man when he sees him, and hypocrites will fool no one at all" (vv. 5–6 TLB).

Not only will their character and motives be exposed and judged, but so will their ungodly methods (v. 7). No longer will the poor and helpless be cheated by these liars! Instead of knaves, the leaders who rule with Messiah will be noble people who plan noble things.

Behind the selfish rulers of Judah, and influencing them for evil, were the "aristocratic women" of Jerusalem, who were complacent and self-confident in a time of grave national crisis (vv. 9–14; see 3:16–26; Amos 4:1–3; 6:1–6). Isaiah warned them that "in little more than a year" (NIV), the land and the cities would be desolate. This took place in 701 BC when Sennacherib's Assyrian army invaded Judah and devastated the land. The Jews confined in Jerusalem were greatly concerned about future harvests, and Isaiah had a word for them (Isa. 37:30–31). But before the siege ended and God delivered Jerusalem, these worldly women in Jerusalem had to sacrifice not only their luxuries, but also their necessities.

In 32:15–20, the prophet returned to his description of the messianic kingdom and emphasized the restoration of peace and prosperity. None of these changes took place after the deliverance of Jerusalem in 701 BC or when the remnant returned to Jerusalem from Babylon, so we must assign these prophecies to the future kingdom. Because of the outpouring of the Holy Spirit, there will be peace and plenty because there will be righteousness in the land (Joel 2:28–32; Zech. 12:10; Ezek. 36:26–27). The land will be so productive that the desert will be like a fruitful field and the fruitful field like a forest. The people will fear no enemies, and their work will be rewarded.

Judah could have enjoyed safety, quietness, and assurance had they trusted wholly in the Lord and not turned to Egypt for help (Isa. 30:15–18; 32:17–18). *Righteousness* is the key word in verse 17, for there can be no true peace without a right relationship with God (Rom. 5:1; James 3:13–17). When sinners trust Christ and receive the gift of righteousness, then they can have peace in their hearts and peace with one another.

## 2. Jerusalem Will Be Delivered (33:1–24)

This is the sixth and final "woe" in this section (28:1; 29:1, 15; 30:1; 31:1), and it is directed against Sennacherib because of his treachery against Judah. In unbelief, King Hezekiah had tried to "buy off" the Assyrians (2 Kings 18:13–15), but Sennacherib had broken the agreement and invaded Judah anyway. He was a thief, a traitor, and a tyrant; and God promised to judge him. He had destroyed others, so he would be destroyed. He had dealt treacherously with nations, so they would deal treacherously with him. God is not mocked; sinners reap what they have sown (Gal. 6:7).

Isaiah 33:2 is the prayer of the godly remnant when Jerusalem was surrounded by the Assyrian army. Isaiah had promised that God would be gracious to them if they would only trust Him (30:18–19), so a few devout people turned His promise into prayer. God spared Jerusalem for David's sake (37:35) and because a believing remnant trusted God and prayed. Never underestimate the power of a praying minority.

Assyria was proud of her power and the spoils she had gathered in battle. The Assyrian army swept through the land like devouring locusts, but that would change. The day would come when Judah would strip the dead Assyrian army and Sennacherib would be assassinated in the temple of the god he claimed was stronger than Jehovah (vv. 36–38).

The Lord was exalted in the defeat of Assyria (33:5), for no human wisdom or power could have done what He did. We must remember that nations and individuals can have stability in uncertain times only when they trust God and seek His wisdom and glory. King Hezekiah did a foolish thing when he took the temple treasures and tried to bribe Sennacherib (2 Kings 18:13–16), but God forgave him and reminded him that "the fear of the LORD is [your] treasure" (Isa. 33:6). <u>Unbelief looks to human</u> resources for help, but faith looks to God.

During the time of the Assyrian invasion, the situation in Judah was grim (vv. 7–9). Judah's bravest soldiers wept when they saw one city after another fall to the enemy. The official Jewish envoys wept because their negotiations accomplished nothing. The roads were dangerous, the fields and orchards were ruined, and there was no way of escape.

Except for—God! "'Now will I rise,' saith the LORD, 'now will I be exalted; now will I lift up myself'" (v. 10). In verses 11–12, Isaiah used several images to describe God's judgment on the Assyrians. The Assyrians were "pregnant" with all sorts of plans to conquer Jerusalem, but they would give birth to chaff and straw, and their plans would amount to nothing. Their army was panting to attack, but their hot breath would only become a fire that would destroy them like dead bones or cut bushes. God is longsuffering with His enemies, but when He decides to judge, He does a thorough job.

The account of the amazing deliverance of Jerusalem was told far and wide, and the Gentile nations had to acknowledge the greatness of Jehovah, the God of the Jews. Some scholars believe that Psalm 126 grew out of this experience and may have been written by Hezekiah. "Then they said among the nations, 'The LORD hath done great things for them'" (v. 2 NKJV). We witness to a lost world when we trust Him and let Him have His way.

The <u>miracle deliverance of Jerusalem not only brought glory to God among the Gentiles, but it also brought fear and conviction to the Jews</u> (Isa. 33:14–16). God does not deliver us so that we are free to return to our sins. "But there is forgiveness with thee, that thou mayest be feared" (Ps. 130:4)! When Jews in Jerusalem saw 185,000 Assyrian soldiers slain by God in one night, they realized anew that the God of Israel was "a consuming fire" (Isa. 10:17; Heb. 12:29). Were they even safe in Jerusalem?

Isaiah 33:15 describes the kind of person God will accept and bless (see also Ps. 15; 24). By ourselves, we cannot achieve these qualities of character; they come only as we trust Jesus Christ and grow in grace. Many religious people in Jerusalem had hearts far from God because their religion was only a matter of external ceremonies (Isa. 29:13). Isaiah hoped that the miracle deliverance of the city would bring these people to a place of true devotion to the Lord. It is only as we walk with the Lord that we have real security and satisfaction.

In 33:17–24, the prophet lifts his vision to the end times and saw Jerusalem ruled by King Messiah. God's victory over Assyria was but a "dress rehearsal" for His victory over the whole Gentile world system that will one day assemble to destroy the Holy City (Zech. 14:1–9). When our Lord was ministering on earth, the unbelieving Jews said, "There is no beauty that we should desire him" (Isa. 53:2). But when they see Him and believe, then they will perceive His great beauty (Zech. 12:3—13:1; Ps. 45).

In contrast to the ordeal of the Assyrian siege, the Jews in the messianic kingdom will experience no terror, see no arrogant military officers, and hear no foreign speech (Isa. 33:18–19). Jerusalem will be like a tent that will not be moved (see 54:1–3), pitched by a broad river that will never carry the vessels of invading armies. Jerusalem is one of the few great cities of antiquity that was not built near a river, but that will change during the millennial kingdom (Ezek. 47). Of course, the river symbolizes the peace that the Lord gives to His people (Isa. 48:18; 66:12; Ps. 46:4).

Jerusalem was a ship that almost sank (Isa. 33:23), but the Lord brought it through the storm (Ps. 107:23–32), and the weakest of the Jews was able to take spoils from the dead army. "All the functions of government—judicial, legislative, and executive—will be centered in the Messianic King," says the note on Isaiah 33:22 in *The New Scofield Reference Bible*. No wonder His people can say, "He will save us!"

Both sickness and sin will be absent from the city. The Messiah will be their Redeemer and Savior, and the nation "shall be forgiven their iniquity"

(v. 24). In Isaiah's day, the Jews were a "sinful nation, a people laden with iniquity" (1:4), just as lost sinners are today, but when they see Him and trust Him, their sins will be washed away. If you have never heeded the gracious invitation of Isaiah 1:18, do so today!

### 3. THE SINFUL WORLD WILL BE JUDGED (34:1–17)

Israel's ancient enemy Edom is singled out in verses 5–6, but this divine judgment will come upon the whole world. Edom is only one example of God's judgment on the Gentile nations because of what they have done to His people Israel. "For the LORD has a day of vengeance, a year of retribution, to uphold Zion's cause" (v. 8 NIV). In the day of the Lord, the Gentiles will be repaid for the way they have treated the Jews and exploited their land (Joel 3:1–17). "Zion's cause" may not get much support among the nations today, but God will come to their defense and make their cause succeed.

Isaiah began this section with a military picture of the armies on earth (Isa. 34:2–3) and in heaven (v. 4). The enemy armies on earth will be slaughtered, the land will be drenched with blood, and the bodies of the slain will be left unburied to rot and to smell. This is a vivid description of the battle of Armageddon (Rev. 19:11–21), the humiliating defeat and destruction of the armies of the world that dare to attack the Son of God. The hosts of heaven will also be affected by vast cosmic disturbances (Isa. 34:4; see Matt. 24:29; Joel 2:10, 30–31; 3:15; Rev. 6:13–14). What a day that will be!

In Isaiah 34:5–8, the prophet moved from the battlefield to the temple and saw the worldwide judgment as a great sacrifice that God offers (see Jer. 46:10; 50:27; Ezek. 39:17–19). The practice was for the people to kill the sacrifices and offer them to God, but now it is God who offers the wicked as sacrifices. Bozrah was an important city in Edom; the name means "grape-gathering" (see Isa. 63:1–8). God sees His enemies as animals: rams, goats, lambs, oxen, and bulls to be sacrificed, along with the fat (Lev. 3:9–11). These nations sacrificed the Jews, so God used them for sacrifices.

The picture changes again, and Isaiah compared the day of the Lord to the judgment of Sodom and Gomorrah (Isa. 34:9–10; Gen. 18—19). This is a significant comparison because, just before the coming of the Lord, society will be "as it was in the days of Lot" (Luke 17:28). Tar running like streams and sulfur like dust will keep the fires of judgment burning (Gen. 14:10; 19:24). The description in Isaiah 34:10 reminds us of the fall of Babylon (Rev. 14:8–11; 19:3). We should also remember that the fires of eternal hell, the lake of fire, will never be quenched (Mark 9:43–48).

While Isaiah focused especially on Edom (Isa. 34:5–6), he was using that proud nation as an example of what God would do to all the Gentile nations during the day of the Lord. When God finishes His work, the land will be a wilderness, occupied by brambles and thorns, wild beasts, and singular birds (vv. 11–17). God will see to it that each bird will have a mate to reproduce, and no humans will be around to drive them from their nests.

"But the day of the Lord will come as a thief in the night" (2 Peter 3:10). Why is God waiting? Because God "is longsuffering toward us, not willing that any should perish but that all should come to repentance" (2 Peter 3:9 NKJV). How much longer God will wait, nobody knows; so it behooves lost sinners to repent today and trust the Savior.

## 4. The Glorious Kingdom Will Be Established (35:1–10)

But the wilderness will not remain a wilderness, for the Lord will transform the earth into a Garden of Eden. All of nature eagerly looks for the coming of the Lord (55:12–13; Rom. 8:19; Ps. 96:11–13; 98:7–9), for nature knows that it will be set free from the curse of sin (Gen. 3:17–19) and share the glory of the kingdom. Lebanon, Carmel, and Sharon were three of the most fruitful and beautiful places in the land, and yet the desert would become more fruitful and beautiful than the three places put together! There will be no more "parched ground" (Isa. 35:7), because the land will become a garden of glory.

Isaiah used the promise of the coming kingdom to strengthen those in his day who were weak and afraid (vv. 3–4). In the kingdom, there will be no more blind or deaf, lame or dumb; for all will be made whole to enjoy a glorious new world. (In 32:3–4, the prophet wrote about spiritual deficiencies, but here he is describing physical handicaps.) Our Lord referred to these verses when He sent a word of encouragement to John the Baptist (Luke 7:18–23). The King was on earth and sharing with needy people the blessings of the coming kingdom.

Isaiah 35:8 expresses one of Isaiah's favorite themes: the highway (11:16; 19:23; 40:3; 62:10). During the Assyrian invasion, the highways were not safe (33:8), but during the kingdom age it will be safe to travel. There will be one special highway: "The Way of Holiness." In ancient cities, there were often special roads that only kings and priests could use, but when the Messiah reigns, all of His people will be invited to use this highway. Isaiah pictures God's redeemed, ransomed, and rejoicing Jewish families going up to the yearly feasts in Jerusalem, to praise their Lord.

When Isaiah spoke and wrote these words, it is likely that the Assyrians had ravaged the land, destroyed the crops, and made the highways unsafe for travel. The people were cooped up in Jerusalem, wondering what would happen next. The members of the faithful remnant were trusting God's promises and praying for God's help, and God answered their prayers. If God kept His promises to His people centuries ago and delivered them, will He not keep His promises in the future and establish His glorious kingdom for His chosen people? Of course He will!

The future is your friend when Jesus Christ is your Savior and Lord.

# QUESTIONS FOR PERSONAL REFLECTION
# OR GROUP DISCUSSION

1. As you read or watch the news, which trends and predictions cause you concern and anxiety?

2. How might even negative trends be translated into opportunities for the body of Christ locally, nationally, or globally?

3. Describe the future for God's people as depicted in Isaiah 32—35.

4. What new crises might God's planned future for His people produce?

5. What new activities occur in the messianic kingdom, according to Isaiah?

6. Read Luke 4:16–21. How does Jesus' announcement (from Isaiah 61) summarize the new kingdom's activities?

7. What do you think is the significance of Jesus' statement, "Today this Scripture is fulfilled in your hearing"?

8. In what ways is the kingdom of God both "here" and "yet to come"?

9. In light of the new kingdom activities, what should our priorities be as kingdom people?

10. How can we as Christians begin to anticipate and prepare for the future rather than simply reacting to it when it comes?

# KING HEZEKIAH

## (Isaiah 36—39)

Except for David and Solomon, no king of Judah is given more attention or commendation in Scripture than Hezekiah. Eleven chapters are devoted to him in 2 Kings 18—20; 2 Chronicles 29—32; and Isaiah 36—39. "He trusted in the LORD God of Israel; so that after him was none like him among all the kings of Judah, nor any that were before him" (2 Kings 18:5).

He began his reign about 715 BC, though he may have been coregent with his father as early as 729 BC. He restored the temple facilities and services of worship, destroyed the idols and the high places (hill shrines where the people falsely worshipped Jehovah), and sought to bring the people back to vital faith in the Lord. He led the people in a nationwide two-week celebration of Passover and invited Jews from the northern kingdom to participate. "And in every work that he began in the service of the house of God, and in the law, and in the commandments, to see his God, he did it with all his heart, and prospered" (2 Chron. 31:21).

After the fall of the northern kingdom in 722 BC, Judah had constant problems with Assyria. Hezekiah finally rebelled against Assyria (2 Kings 18:7), and when Sennacherib threatened to attack, Hezekiah tried to bribe him with tribute (vv. 13–16). It was a lapse of faith on Hezekiah's part that God could not bless. Sennacherib accepted the treasures but broke the treaty (Isa. 33:1) and invaded Judah in 701 BC. The account of God's miraculous deliverance of His people is given in Isaiah 36—37.

Bible students generally agree that Hezekiah's sickness (Isa. 38) and foolish reception of the envoys (Isa. 39) took place before the Assyrian invasion, possibly between the time Hezekiah sent the tribute and Sennacherib broke the treaty. Then why are these chapters not arranged chronologically?

The prophet arranged the account as a "bridge" between the two parts of his book. Chapters 36 and 37 end the first part of the book with its emphasis on Assyria, and chapters 38 and 39 introduce the second part of the book, with its emphasis on Babylon. Isaiah mentioned Babylon earlier in his book (13:1ff.; 31:1ff.), but this is the first time he clearly predicts Judah's captivity in Babylon.

Chapters 36—39 teach us some valuable lessons about faith, prayer, and the dangers of pride. Though the setting today may be different, the problems and temptations are still the same; for Hezekiah's history is our history, and Hezekiah's God is our God.

# Chapter Eight

# GOD SAVE THE KING!

## (Isaiah 36—39)

Former U.S. Secretary of State Dr. Henry Kissinger once told the *New York Times*, "There cannot be a crisis next week. My schedule is already full."

Crises come, whether schedules permit them or not, and sometimes crises seem to pile up. How do we handle them? What life does to us depends on what life finds in us. A crisis does not make a person; it shows what a person is made of.

Hezekiah faced three crises in a short time: an international crisis (the invasion of the Assyrian army), a personal crisis (sickness and near death), and a national crisis (the visit of the Babylonian envoys). He came through the first two victoriously, but the third one tripped him up. Hezekiah was a great and godly man, but he was still a man, and that meant he had all the frailties of human flesh. However, before we find fault with him, we had better examine our own lives to see how successfully we have handled our own tests.

## 1. THE INVASION CRISIS (36:1—37:38; 2 KINGS 18—19; 2 CHRON. 32)

Crises often come when circumstances seem to be at their best. Hezekiah had led the nation in a great reformation, and the people were reunited in the fear of the Lord. They had put away their idols, restored the temple services, and sought the blessing of their God. But instead of receiving blessing, they found themselves facing battles! "After all that Hezekiah had so faithfully done, Sennacherib king of Assyria came and invaded Judah" (2 Chron. 32:1 NIV).

Had God turned a blind eye and a deaf ear to all that Hezekiah and his people had done? Of course not! The Assyrian invasion was a part of God's discipline to teach His people to trust Him alone. Even Hezekiah had at first put his trust in treaties and treasures (2 Kings 18:13–16), only to learn that the enemy will keep the wealth but not keep his word. Judah had negotiated to get help from Egypt, an act of unbelief that Isaiah severely rebuked (Isa. 30:1–7; 31:1–3). God's great purpose in the life of faith is to build godly character. Hezekiah and his people needed to learn that faith is living without scheming.

The Assyrians had ravaged Judah and were now at Lachish, about thirty miles southwest of Jerusalem. According to 2 Kings 18:17, Sennacherib sent three of his most important officers to arrange for Hezekiah's surrender of the city: Tartan ("Supreme Commander"), Rabsaris ("Chief Officer"), and Rabshakeh ("Field Commander"). These are military titles, not personal names. The three men were met by three of Judah's leading officials: Eliakim, Shebna (see Isa. 22:15–25), and Joah (36:3).

The place of their meeting is significant, for it is the very place where Isaiah confronted Ahaz, Hezekiah's father, some thirty years before (7:3). Ahaz had refused to trust the Lord but had instead made a treaty with Assyria (2 Kings 16:5–9), and now the Assyrians were ready to take Jerusalem! Isaiah had warned Ahaz what Assyria would do (Isa. 7:17–25), and his words were now fulfilled.

**Reproach (Isa. 36:4–21).** The field commander's speech is one of the most insolent and blasphemous found anywhere in Scripture, for he reproached the God of Israel (37:4, 17, 23–24). He emphasized the "greatness" of the king of Assyria (36:4, 13) because he knew the common people were listening and he wanted to frighten them (vv. 11–12). His speech is a masterful piece of psychological warfare in which he discredits everything that the Jews held dear. The key word is *trust*, used seven times (vv. 4–7, 9, 15). "In what is your confidence?" asked the field commander. "You can have no confidence, for everything you trust in has failed!"

He began with their strategy. They had turned to Egypt for help, but Egypt was only a broken reed. (Isaiah had said the same thing! See 30:1–7; 31:1–3.) As for trusting the Lord, that was sure to fail. Hezekiah had incurred the Lord's displeasure by removing the high places and altars and requiring everybody to worship at Jerusalem. (What did a heathen soldier know about the worship of the true God?) So, according to the field commander, Judah had no help on earth (Egypt) or in heaven (the Lord). They were already defeated!

What about their military resources? Hezekiah had fortified Jerusalem (2 Chron. 32:2–8), but the field commander laughed at Judah's military might. Judah had neither the men, the horses, nor the chariots to attack the Assyrians. Even if Assyria provided the equipment, the Jewish soldiers were too weak to defeat the least of the enemy's officers. All the chariots and horsemen of Egypt could never defeat Sennacherib's great army. (Isaiah would agree with him again; see Isa. 30:15–17.) *final blow*

The field commander's coup de grace was that everything Assyria had done was according to the will of the Lord (36:10). How could Judah fight against its own God? In one sense, this statement was true; for God is in charge of the nations of the world (10:5–6; Dan. 4:17, 25, 32; 5:21). But no nation can do what it pleases and use God for the excuse, as Sennacherib and his army would soon find out. *Nebuchadnezzar*

According to the field commander, Judah could not trust in its strategy, its military resources, or in its God. Nor could its people trust in their king (Isa. 36:13–20). The king of Assyria was a "great king," but Hezekiah was a nobody who was deceiving the people. Instead of trusting Hezekiah's promise of help from the Lord, the people should trust Sennacherib's promise of a comfortable home in Assyria. The people knew that their farms, orchards, and vineyards had been ruined by the Assyrian army, and that Judah was facing a bleak future. If they stayed in Jerusalem, they might starve to death. Perhaps they should surrender and keep themselves and their families alive.

Hezekiah and Isaiah had told the people to trust the Lord, but the field commander reminded the people that the gods of the other nations had not succeeded in protecting or delivering them. (Hezekiah knew why; see 37:18–19.) Even Samaria was defeated, and they worshipped the same God as Judah. To the field commander, Jehovah was just another god, and Sennacherib did not need to worry about Him.

God summons us to walk by faith and not by sight (2 Cor. 5:7). To those Jews in Jerusalem who were living in unbelief, the field commander's arguments must have seemed reasonable, and his evidence compelling. But God had promised to deliver His people from the Assyrian army, and His word would stand.

**Repentance (Isa. 36:22—37:20).** By the king's orders, nobody replied to the field commander's speech. Insolence is best answered with silence. Jerusalem's deliverance did not depend on negotiating with the enemy but on trusting the Lord.

Hezekiah and his officers humbled themselves before the Lord and sought His face. As the king went into the temple, perhaps he recalled the promise God had given to Solomon after he had dedicated the temple: "If my people, which are called by my name, shall humble themselves, and pray, and seek my face, and turn from their wicked ways; then will I hear from heaven, and will forgive their sin, and will heal their land" (2 Chron. 7:14).

Even though the Lord had brought Assyria to chasten Judah (Isa. 7:17–25), He had determined that Jerusalem would not be taken by the enemy (10:5–34). Previous to the invasion, when Hezekiah had been deathly ill, Isaiah had assured him of deliverance (38:4–6). God's promises are sure, but God's people must claim them by faith before God can work.

So the king sent word to Isaiah, asking him to pray, and the king himself called out to the Lord for help.

In the building up of our faith, the Word of God and prayer go together (Rom. 10:17). That is why Isaiah sent the king a message from the Lord. His word of encouragement had three points: (1) do not be afraid, (2) the Assyrians will depart, and (3) the "great king" will die in Assyria.

When the three Assyrian officers returned to headquarters, they learned that an Egyptian army was on its way to help defend Hezekiah. Sennacherib did not want to fight a war on two fronts, so he started to put more pressure on Jerusalem to surrender immediately. This threatening message came to Hezekiah in the form of a letter, and he took it to the temple and "spread it before the Lord."

Hezekiah's prayer (Isa. 37:15–20) is saturated with biblical theology and is not unlike the prayer of the church in Acts 4:24–31. He affirmed his faith in the one true and living God, and he worshipped Him. Jehovah is "Lord of Hosts," that is, "Lord of the armies" (Ps. 46:7, 11). He is the Creator of all things (96:5) and knows what is going on in His creation. His eyes can see our plight, and His ears can hear our plea (see Ps. 115). King Hezekiah did not want deliverance merely for his people's sake, but that God alone might be glorified (Isa. 37:20; Ps. 46:10).

**Reply (Isa. 37:21–35).** God's response to this prayer was to send King Hezekiah another threefold message of assurance: Jerusalem would not be taken (vv. 22, 31–35); the Assyrians would depart (vv. 23–29); and the Jews would not starve (v. 30).

*(1) Jerusalem would be delivered (vv. 22, 31–35).* The "daughter of Zion" was still a virgin; she had not been ravaged by the enemy. She could look at the Assyrians and shake her head in scorn, for they could not touch her. God would spare His remnant and plant them once more in the land.

Why did God deliver His people, when so many of them were not faithful to Him? First, to glorify His own name (vv. 23, 35), the very thing about which Hezekiah had prayed (v. 20). God defended Jerusalem for His name's sake, because Sennacherib had reproached the Holy One of Israel. The Assyrians had exalted themselves above men and gods, but they could not exalt themselves above Jehovah God, the Holy One of Israel!

God also saved Jerusalem because of His covenant with David (v. 35; 2 Sam. 7). Jerusalem was the City of David, and God had promised that one of David's descendants would reign on the throne forever. This was fulfilled ultimately in Jesus Christ (Luke 1:32–33), but God did keep David's lamp burning in Jerusalem as long as He could (1 Kings 11:13, 36).

The Jewish nation had an important mission to fulfill in bringing the Savior into the world, and no human army could thwart the purposes of Almighty God. Even though only a remnant of Jews might remain, God would use His people to accomplish His divine purposes and fulfill His promise to Abraham that all the world would be blessed through him (Gen. 12:1–3).

*(2) The Assyrians would depart (vv. 23–29).* God addressed the proud Assyrian king and reminded him of all the boastful words he and his servants had spoken. "I" and "my" occur seven times in this passage. It reminds us of Lucifer's words in 14:12–17 and our Lord's parable in Luke 12:13–21. "Pride goes before destruction, and a haughty spirit before a fall" (Prov. 16:18 NKJV).

Sennacherib boasted of his military might and his great conquests, for no obstacle stood in his way. If he so desired, like a god, he could even dry up the rivers! But the king of Assyria forgot that he was only God's tool for accomplishing His purposes on the earth, and the tool must not boast against the Maker (Isa. 10:5–19). God would humble Sennacherib and his army by treating them like cattle and leading them away from Jerusalem (37:7, 29).

*(3) The people would not starve (v. 30).* We do not know the month in which these events occurred, but it may have been past the time for sowing

a new crop. Before the people could get the land back to its normal productivity, they would have to eat what grew of itself from previous crops, and that would take faith. They would also need to renovate their farms after all the damage the Assyrians had done. But the same God who delivered them would provide for them. It would be like the years before and after the Year of Jubilee (Lev. 25:1–24).

Some Bible scholars believe that Psalm 126 was written to commemorate Jerusalem's deliverance from the Assyrian army. The psalm surely is not referring to the Jews' deliverance from the Babylonian captivity, because that was not a sudden event that surprised both Jews and Gentiles, nor did the Gentiles praise Jehovah for delivering Israel from Babylon. Psalm 126 fits best with the events described in Isaiah 36 and 37.

The harvest promise in verse 30 parallels Psalm 126:5–6. The seed would certainly be precious in those days! That grain could be used for making bread for the family, but the father must use it for seed; so it is no wonder he weeps. Yet God promised a harvest, and He kept His promise. The people did not starve.

**Retaliation (Isa. 37:36–38).** The field commander had joked that one Assyrian junior officer was stronger than 2,000 Jewish charioteers (36:8–9), but it took only one of God's angels to destroy 185,000 Assyrian soldiers (see Ex. 12:12; 2 Sam. 24:15–17)! Isaiah had prophesied the destruction of the Assyrian army. God would mow them down like a forest (Isa. 10:33–34), devastate them with a storm (30:27–30), and throw them into the fire like garbage on the city dump (vv. 31–33).

But that was not all. After Sennacherib left Judah a defeated man, he returned to his capital city of Nineveh. Twenty years later, as a result of a power struggle among his sons, Sennacherib was assassinated by two of his sons in fulfillment of Isaiah's prophecy (37:7), and it happened in the temple of his god! The field commander had ridiculed the gods of the nations, but Sennacherib's own god could not protect him.

## 2. THE ILLNESS CRISIS (38:1–22; 2 KINGS 20:1–11)

**Peril (Isa. 38:1).** As mentioned before, this event took place before the Assyrian invasion, though the invasion was impending (see v. 6). When the president or prime minister of a country is sick or injured, it affects everything from the stock market to the news coverage. Imagine how the people of Judah reacted when they heard that the king was going to die—and Assyria was on the march! If their godly leader died, who would govern them?

But there was even more involved. Apparently, Hezekiah did not have a son and therefore would have to appoint a near relative to take the throne of David. Would God's promise to David fail (2 Sam. 7:16)? And why would it fail at a time of national calamity?

**Prayer (Isa. 38:2–3).** The king did not turn to the wall in a sulking manner, like Ahab (1 Kings 21:4), but in order to have privacy for his praying. It may be too that he was turning his face toward the temple (8:28–30). Some have criticized Hezekiah for weeping and praying, saying that his prayer was selfish, but most of us would have prayed the same way. It is a natural thing for us to want to live and continue serving God. Furthermore, Hezekiah was burdened for the future of the throne and the nation.

Hezekiah did not ask God to spare him because he had been such a faithful servant (Isa. 38:3). That would be a subtle form of bribery. Rather, he asked God to spare him so he could continue to serve and complete the spiritual restoration of the nation. Certainly he was concerned about his own life, as any of us would be, but he also had a burden for his people.

**Promise (Isa. 38:4–8).** The request was granted quickly, for Isaiah had not gone very far from the sick room when the Lord gave him the answer (2 Kings 20:4). The prophet became the king's physician and told the attendants what medicine to apply (Isa. 38:21). God can heal by using any means He desires. Isaiah also told the king that his life would be prolonged for fifteen years. The king asked confirmation of the promise (v. 22), and God gave him a sign. The sundial was probably a pillar whose shadow marked the hours on a double set of stairs. In another promise, Isaiah assured the king that the Assyrians would not capture Jerusalem.

**Pondering (Isa. 38:9–20).** Hezekiah was an author of psalms (v. 20) and supervised a group of scholars who copied the Old Testament Scriptures (Prov. 25:1). In this beautiful meditation, the king tells us how he felt during his experience of illness and recovery. He had some new experiences that transformed him.

For one thing, God gave him a new appreciation of life (Isa. 38:9–12). We take life for granted till it is about to be taken from us, and then we cling to it as long as we can. Hezekiah pictured death as the end of the journey (vv. 11–12), a tent taken down (v. 12a; see 2 Cor. 5:1–8), and a weaving cut from the loom (Isa. 38:12b). Life was hanging by a thread!

He also had a new appreciation of prayer (vv. 13–14). Were it not for prayer, Hezekiah could not have made it. At night the king felt like a frail animal being attacked by a fierce lion, and in the daytime he felt like a helpless bird. During this time of suffering, Hezekiah examined his own heart and confessed his sins, and God forgave him (v. 17). *Undertake for me* means "Be my surety. Stand with me!"

The king ended with a new appreciation of opportunities for service (vv. 15–20). There was a new humility in his walk, a deeper love for the Lord in his heart, and a new song of praise on his lips. He had a new determination to praise God all the days of his life, for now those days were very important to him. "So teach us to number our days, that we may apply our hearts unto wisdom" (Ps. 90:12).

There are some students who feel that Hezekiah was wrong in asking God to spare his life. Three years later, his son Manasseh was born (2 Kings 21:1), and he reigned for fifty-five years, the most wicked king in the entire dynasty! Had Hezekiah died without an heir, this would not have happened. But we have no guarantee that any other successor would have been any better, and Manasseh's grandson was godly King Josiah, who did much to bring the nation back to the Lord. Manasseh did repent after God chastened him, and he ended his years serving the Lord (2 Chron. 33:11–20). It is unwise for us to second-guess God or history.

## 3. The Investigation Crisis (39:1–8)

The news about Hezekiah's sickness and recovery had spread widely so that even people in Babylon knew about it (2 Chron. 32:23). Hezekiah was a famous man, and other nations would be concerned about him and want to court his favor. The stability of Judah was important to the balance of power in that day. At this time, Babylon was not a great world power, and few people would have thought that Assyria would one day collapse and be replaced by Babylon. Of course, God knew, but Hezekiah did not seek His guidance.

The stated reason for the diplomatic mission was to honor Hezekiah and officially rejoice at his recovery. But the real reason was to obtain information about the financial resources of the nation of Judah. After all, Babylon might need some of that wealth in their future negotiations or battles. It is also likely that Hezekiah was seeking Babylon's assistance against Assyria.

When Satan cannot defeat us as the "roaring lion" (1 Peter 5:8–9), he comes as the deceiving serpent (2 Cor. 11:3). What Assyria could not do with weapons, Babylon did with gifts. God permitted the enemy to test Hezekiah so that the proud king might learn what was really in his heart (2 Chron. 32:31).

It was certainly a mistake for Hezekiah to show his visitors all his wealth, but pride made him do it. After a time of severe suffering, sometimes it feels so good just to feel good that we let down our guard and fail to watch and pray. The king was basking in fame and wealth and apparently neglecting his spiritual life. Hezekiah was safer as a sick man in bed than as a healthy man on the throne. Had he consulted first with Isaiah, the king would have avoided blundering as he did.

The prophet reminded Hezekiah that, as king, he was only the steward of Judah's wealth and not the owner (Isa. 39:6). Some of that wealth had come from previous kings, and Hezekiah could claim no credit for it. All of us are mere stewards of what God has given to us, and we have no right to boast about anything. "For who makes you differ from another? And what do you have that you did not receive? Now if you did indeed receive it, why do you boast as if you had not received it?" (1 Cor. 4:7 NKJV). "A man can receive nothing unless it has been given to him from heaven" (John 3:27 NKJV).

Isaiah 39:7 is Isaiah's first explicit announcement of the future Babylonian captivity of Judah. In spite of Hezekiah's reforms, the nation decayed spiritually during the next century, and in 586 BC Babylon destroyed Jerusalem and took the people captive. Hezekiah's sin was not the cause of this judgment, for the sins of rulers, priests, and false prophets mounted up from year to year till God could take it no longer (2 Chron. 36:13–16).

Is Hezekiah's response in Isaiah 39:8 an expression of relief that he escaped trouble? If so, it would certainly be heartless on his part to rejoice that future generations would suffer what he should have suffered! His statement is more likely an expression of his humble acceptance of God's will, and 2 Chronicles 32:26 bears this out. The king did humble himself before God, and God forgave him.

Even the greatest and most godly of the Lord's servants can become proud and disobey God, so we must pray for Christian leaders that they will stay humble before their Master. But if any of His servants do sin, the Lord is willing to forgive when they sincerely repent and confess to Him (1 John 1:9). "A broken and a contrite heart, O God, thou wilt not despise" (Ps. 51:17).

# QUESTIONS FOR PERSONAL REFLECTION
# OR GROUP DISCUSSION

1. What difference do you notice when you face crises in the Spirit's power versus in your own strength?

2. How typical do you think Hezekiah's responses were to the crises he faced?

3. How does pride often affect our response to crises and conflicts?

4. What alternative solutions could Hezekiah have chosen to deal with the crisis?

5. What solutions would you recommend to the king, and why?

6. What principles can you glean from Hezekiah's experiences that would motivate you to become a person of prayer and one who trusts God?

7. What do you think about Hezekiah's prayer for healing (see Isa. 38:1–5)?

8. If God's answer to Hezekiah's plea for healing had been "no" rather than "yes," how might God's purposes still have been accomplished in that crisis?

9. Read Galatians 5:22–23. Which of the fruits of the Spirit seem to come easier for you? For which of these do you have to trust the Lord on a regular basis? Which one of these fruits of the Spirit are you asking God to increase in your life?

10. As you think back on Hezekiah's experiences, what lessons on prayer, faith, and pride do you want to remember?

# "THE BOOK OF CONSOLATION"

## (Isaiah 40—66)

The book of Isaiah can be called "a Bible in miniature." There are sixty-six chapters in Isaiah and sixty-six books in the Bible. The thirty-nine chapters of the first part of Isaiah may be compared to the Old Testament with its thirty-nine books, and both focus primarily on God's judgment of sin. The twenty-seven chapters of the second part may be seen to parallel the twenty-seven books of the New Testament, and both emphasize the grace of God.

The "New Testament" section of Isaiah opens with the ministry of John the Baptist (40:3–5; Mark 1:1–4) and closes with the new heavens and the new earth (Isa. 65:17; 66:22), and in between there are many references to the Lord Jesus Christ as Savior and King. Of course, the chapter divisions in Isaiah are not a part of the original inspired text, but the comparison is still interesting.

In the "New Testament" section of Isaiah, the prophet is particularly addressing a future generation of Jews. In chapters 1—39 his audience was his own generation, and his primary message was that God would defend Jerusalem and defeat the Assyrian invaders. But in chapters 40—66 the prophet looks far ahead and sees Babylon destroying Jerusalem and the Jews going into captivity. (This happened in 586 BC.) But he also saw God forgiving His people, delivering them from captivity, and taking them back to Jerusalem to rebuild the temple and restore the nation.

The primary world figure in Isaiah 1—39 is Sennacherib, king of Assyria; but in chapters 40—66 the world leader is Cyrus, king of Persia. It was Cyrus who defeated the Babylonians and in 541 BC issued the decree that permitted the Jews to return to their land to rebuild the city and the temple (Ezra 1:1–4). When Isaiah wrote these messages, Babylon was not yet a great world power, but the prophet was inspired by God to see the course the international scene would take.

Chapters 40—66 may be divided into three parts (40—48; 49—57; and 58—66), with the same statement separating the first two sections: "There is no peace, saith the LORD, unto the wicked" (48:22; 57:21). Chapters 40—48 emphasize the greatness of God the Father in contrast to the vanity of the heathen idols; chapters 49—57 extol the graciousness of God the Son, the Suffering Servant; and chapters 58—66 describe the glory of God in the future kingdom, and the emphasis is on the work of the Holy Spirit (59:19, 21; 61:1ff.; 63:10–11, 14). Thus, there seems to be a trinitarian structure to these chapters.

The heart of Isaiah 40—66 is chapters 49—57, in which Isaiah exalts the Messiah, God's Suffering Servant. And the heart of chapters 49—57 is 52:13—53:12, the description of the Savior's substitutionary death for the sins of the world. This is the fourth of the "Servant Songs" in Isaiah; the others are 42:1–7; 49:1–6; and 50:1–11. So at the heart of the "New Testament" section of Isaiah's book is our Lord Jesus Christ and His sacrifice on the cross for our sins. No wonder Isaiah has been called "the evangelical prophet."

The Jewish rabbis have called Isaiah 40—66 "The Book of Consolation," and they are right. Isaiah sought to comfort the Jewish remnant in Babylon, after their difficult years of captivity, and to assure them that God was with them and would take them safely home. Along with words of consolation, the prophet also revealed the Messiah, God's Suffering Servant, and described the future regathering of Israel and the promised kingdom. Isaiah saw in Israel's restoration from Babylon a preview of what God would do for them at the end of the age, after the "day of the Lord" and the destruction of the world's last "Babylon" (Rev. 17—19).

So as you study Isaiah 40—66, keep in mind that it was originally addressed to a group of discouraged Jewish refugees who faced a long journey home and a difficult task when they got there. Note how often God says to them, "Fear not!" and how frequently He assures them of His pardon and His presence. It is no surprise that God's people for centuries have turned to these chapters to find assurance and encouragement in the difficult days of life; for in these messages, God says to all of His people, "Be comforted!"

# Chapter Nine

# How Great Thou Art!

## (Isaiah 40—48)

I n your time we have the opportunity to move not only toward the rich society and the powerful society but upward to the Great Society." President Lyndon B. Johnson spoke those words at the University of Michigan on May 22, 1964. Reading them over three decades later, I ask myself, "I wonder how the Jewish captives in Babylon would have responded to what the president said?"

A rich society? They were refugees whose land and Holy City were in ruins.

A powerful society? Without king or army, they were weak and helpless before the nations around them.

A great society? They had been guilty of great rebellion against God and had suffered great humiliation and chastening. They faced a great challenge but lacked great human resources.

That is why the prophet told them to get their eyes off themselves and look by faith to the great God who loved them and promised to do great things for them. "Be not afraid!" he admonished them. "Behold your God!" (40:9).

Years ago, one of my radio listeners sent me a motto that has often encouraged me: "Look at others, and be distressed. Look at yourself, and be depressed. Look to God, and you'll be blessed!" This may not be a piece of literature, but it certainly contains great practical theology. When the outlook is bleak, we need the uplook. "Lift up your eyes on high, and behold who hath created these things ... he is strong in power" (v. 26).

When, like Israel of old, you face a difficult task and an impossible tomorrow, do what they did and remind yourself of the greatness of God. In these nine chapters, the prophet described the greatness of God in three different areas of life.

## 1. GOD IS GREATER THAN OUR CIRCUMSTANCES (40:1–31)

**The circumstances behind us (vv. 1–11).** As the remnant in Babylon looked back, they saw failure and sin, and they needed encouragement. Four voices are heard, each with a special message for these needy people.

*(1) The voice of pardon (vv. 1–2).* The nation had sinned greatly against the Lord, with their idolatry, injustice, immorality, and insensitivity to His messengers (Jer. 7). But they were still His people, and He loved them. Though He would chasten them, He would not forsake them. *Speak tenderly* means "speak to the heart," and *warfare* means "severe trials." "Double" does not suggest that God's chastenings are unfair, for He is merciful even in His punishments (Ezra 9:13). God chastened them in an equivalent measure to what they had done (Jer. 16:18). We should not sin, but if we do, God is waiting to pardon (1 John 1:5—2:2).

*(2) The voice of providence (vv. 3–5).* The Jews had a rough road ahead of them as they returned to rebuild Jerusalem and the temple, but the Lord would go before them to open the way. The picture here is of an ambassador repairing the roads and removing obstacles, preparing the way for the coming of a king. The image of the highway is frequent in Isaiah's prophecy (see 11:16). Of course, the ultimate fulfillment here is in the ministry of John the Baptist as he prepared the way for the ministry of Jesus (Matt. 3:1–6). Spiritually speaking, Israel was in the wilderness when Jesus came,

but when He came, God's glory came (John 1:14). The way back may not be easy, but if we are trusting God, it will be easier.

(3) *The voice of promise (vv. 6–8)*. "All flesh is grass!" Assyria was gone, and now Babylon was gone. Like the grass, nations and their leaders fulfill their purposes and then fade away, but the Word of God abides forever (Ps. 37:1–2; 90:1–6; 103:15–18; 1 Peter 1:24–25). As they began their long journey home, Israel could depend on God's promises. Perhaps they were especially claiming 2 Chronicles 6:36–39.

(4) *The voice of peace (vv. 9–11)*. Now the nation itself comes out of the valley and climbs the mountaintop to declare God's victory over the enemy. To *bring good tidings* means "to preach the good news." The good news in that day was the defeat of Babylon and the release of the captive Jews (52:7–9). The good news today is the defeat of sin and Satan by Jesus Christ and the salvation of all who will trust in Him (61:1–3; Luke 4:18–19). God's arm is a mighty arm for winning the battle (Isa. 40:10), but it is also a loving arm for carrying His weary lambs (v. 11). "We are coming home!" would certainly be good news to the devastated cities of Judah (1:7; 36:1; 37:26).

**The circumstances before us (vv. 12–26).** The Jews were few in number, only a remnant, and facing a long and difficult journey. The victories of Assyria, Babylon, and Persia made it look as though the false gods of the Gentiles were stronger than the God of Israel, but Isaiah reminded the people of the greatness of Jehovah. When you behold the greatness of God, then you will see everything else in life in its proper perspective.

God is greater than anything on earth (vv. 12–20) or anything in heaven (vv. 21–26). Creation shows His wisdom, power, and immensity. He is greater than the nations and their gods. He founded the earth and sits on the throne of heaven, and nothing is equal to our God, let alone greater than our God. The next time you are tempted to think that the world is bigger than God, remember the "drop of a bucket" (v. 15) and the

132 \ Be Comforted

"grasshoppers" (v. 22; see Num. 13:33). And if you ever feel so small that you wonder if God really cares about you personally, remember that He knows the name of every star (Isa. 40:26) and your name as well (see John 10:3, 27)! The same God who numbers and names the stars can heal your broken heart (Ps. 147:3–4).

Someone has defined "circumstances" as "those nasty things you see when you get your eyes off of God." If you look at God through your circumstances, He will seem small and very far away, but if by faith you look at your circumstances through God, He will draw very near and reveal His greatness to you.

**The circumstances within us (vv. 27–31).** Instead of praising the Lord, the nation was complaining to Him that He acted as though He did not know their situation or have any concern for their problems (v. 27; 49:14). Instead of seeing the open door, the Jews saw only the long road before them, and they complained that they did not have strength for the journey. God was asking them to do the impossible.

But God knows how we feel and how we fear, and He is adequate to meet our every need. We can never obey God in our own strength, but we can always trust Him to provide the strength we need (Phil. 4:13). If we trust ourselves, we will faint and fall, but if we wait on the Lord by faith, we will receive strength for the journey. The word *wait* does not suggest that we sit around and do nothing. It means "to hope," to look to God for all that we need (Isa. 26:3; 30:15). This involves meditating on His character and His promises, praying, and seeking to glorify Him.

The word *renew* means "to exchange," as taking off old clothing and putting on new. We exchange our weakness for His power (2 Cor. 12:1–10). As we wait before Him, God enables us to soar when there is a crisis, to run when the challenges are many, and to walk faithfully in the day-by-day demands of life. It is much harder to walk in the ordinary pressures of life than to fly like the eagle in a time of crisis.

"I can plod," said William Carey, the father of modern missions. "That is my only genius. I can persevere in any definite pursuit. To this I owe everything."

The journey of a thousand miles begins with one step. The greatest heroes of faith are not always those who seem to be soaring; often it is they who are patiently plodding. As we wait on the Lord, He enables us not only to fly higher and run faster, but also to walk longer. Blessed are the plodders, for they eventually arrive at their destination!

## 2. GOD IS GREATER THAN OUR FEARS (41:1—44:28)

In this section of the book, the Lord seven times says, "Fear not!" to His people (41:10, 13, 14; 43:1, 5; 44:2, 8), and He says "Fear not!" to us today. As the Jewish remnant faced the challenge of the long journey home and the difficult task of rebuilding, they could think of many causes for fear. But there was one big reason not to be afraid: The Lord was with them and would give them success.

God seeks to calm their fears by assuring them that He is going before them and working on their behalf. The Lord explains a wonderful truth: He has three servants in His employ who will accomplish His will: Cyrus, king of Persia (41:1–7); the nation of Israel (vv. 8–29; 43:1—44:27); and the Messiah (42:1–25).

**(1) God's servant Cyrus (41:1–7).** God convenes the court and asks the nations to present their case against Him, if they can. At least seventeen times in his prophecy, Isaiah writes about "the islands" or "the coastlands" (NIV), referring to the most distant places from the holy land (11:11; 24:15; 41:1, 5; 42:4, 10, 12). "Produce your cause," He challenges these nations (41:21); "present your case" (NIV).

God is not afraid of the nations because He is greater than the nations (40:12–17); He controls their rise and fall. He announced that He would raise up a ruler named Cyrus, who would do His righteous work on earth by defeating other nations for the sake of His people Israel. Cyrus would be a shepherd (44:28) anointed by God (45:1), a ravenous bird that could not be stopped (46:11). "He treads on rulers as if they were mortar, as if he were a potter treading the clay" (41:25 NIV).

Isaiah called Cyrus by name over a century before he was born (590?–529), and while Isaiah nowhere calls Cyrus "God's servant," Cyrus did serve the Lord by fulfilling God's purposes on earth. God handed the nations over to Cyrus and helped him conquer great kings (45:1–4). The enemy was blown away like chaff and dust because the eternal God was leading the army.

As Cyrus moved across the territory east and north of the Holy Land (41:25), the nations were afraid and turned to their idols for help. With keen satire, Isaiah described various workmen helping each other manufacture a god who cannot help them! After all, when the God of heaven is in charge of the conquest, how can men or gods oppose Him?

Cyrus may have thought that he was accomplishing his own plans, but actually he was doing the pleasure of the Lord (44:28). By defeating Babylon, Cyrus made it possible for the Jewish captives to be released and allowed to return to their land to rebuild Jerusalem and the temple (Ezra 1:1–4). "I have raised him up in righteousness, and I will direct all his ways: he shall build my city, and he shall let go my captives" (Isa. 45:13).

Sometimes we forget that God can use even unconverted world leaders for the good of His people and the progress of His work. He raised up Pharaoh in Egypt that He might demonstrate His power (Rom. 9:17), and He even used wicked Herod and cowardly Pontius Pilate to accomplish His plan in the crucifixion of Christ (Acts 4:24–28). "The king's heart is in the hand of the LORD, like the rivers of water; He turns it wherever He wishes" (Prov. 21:1 NKJV).

**(2) God's servant Israel (41:8–29; 43:1—44:28).** The prophet presents four pictures to encourage the people. In contrast to the fear experienced by the Gentile nations is the confidence shown by Israel, God's chosen servant (41:8–13), because God was working on their behalf. In spite of their past rebellion, Israel was not cast away by the Lord. The Jewish captives did not need to fear either Cyrus or Babylon, because Cyrus was working for God, and Babylon would be no more. As you read their paragraph, you sense God's love for His people and His desire to encourage them to trust Him for the future.

The title "My servant" is an honorable one; it was given to great leaders like Moses (Num. 12:7), David (2 Sam. 3:18), the prophets (Jer. 7:25), and the Messiah (Isa. 42:1). But is there any honor in being called a "worm" (41:14–16)? "Servant" defined what they were by God's grace and calling, but "worm" described what they were in themselves. Imagine a worm getting teeth and threshing mountains into dust like chaff! As the nation marched ahead by faith, every mountain and hill would be made low (40:4), and the Lord would turn mountains into molehills!

From the pictures of a servant and a worm, Isaiah turned to the picture of a desert becoming a garden (41:17–20). The image reminds us of Israel's wanderings in the wilderness and God's provision for their every need. Water and trees are important possessions in the East, and God will supply both to His people. Certainly Isaiah was also looking beyond the return from Babylon to the future kingdom when "the desert shall rejoice, and blossom as the rose" (35:1).

The final picture is that of the courtroom (41:21–29). *Produce your cause!* means "Present your case!" God challenged the idols of the nations to prove that they were really gods. Did any of their predictions come true? What have they predicted about the future? Did they announce that Cyrus would appear on the scene or that Jerusalem would be restored? "No one told of this, no one foretold it, no one heard any words from you," taunted the Lord (v. 26 NIV). Not only were the idols unable to make any valid predictions, they were not even able to speak! The judgment of the court was correct: "See, they are all false! Their deeds amount to nothing; their images are but wind and confusion" (v. 29 NIV).

The theme of "Israel God's Servant" is continued in Isaiah 43—44 with an emphasis on God the Redeemer of Israel (43:1–7; note also v. 14; 44:6, 22–24). The word translated "redeem" or "Redeemer" is the Hebrew word for "a kinsman redeemer," a near relative who could free family members and their property from bondage by paying their debts for them. (See Lev. 25:23–28 and the book of Ruth.) God gave Egypt, Ethiopia (Cush), and Seba to Cyrus as a ransom payment to redeem Israel from Babylon, because Israel was so precious to Him. And He gave His own Son as a ransom for lost sinners (Matt. 20:28; 1 Tim. 2:6).

Israel is God's servant in the world and also God's witness to the world (Isa. 43:8–13). This is another courtroom scene where God challenges the idols. "Let them bring in their witnesses!" says the Judge, but of course the idols are helpless and speechless. Twice the Lord says to Israel, "You are My witnesses" (vv. 10, 12 NKJV), for it is in the history of Israel that God has revealed Himself to the world. Frederick the Great asked the Marquis D'Argens, "Can you give me one single irrefutable proof of God?" The marquis replied, "Yes, your majesty, the Jews."

Along with Israel's new freedom and new witness, Isaiah wrote about Israel's new "exodus" (vv. 14–28). Just as God led His people out of Egypt and through the Red Sea (Ex. 12—15), so He will lead them out of Babylon and through the terrible wilderness to their home in the Holy Land. Just as He defeated Pharaoh's army (14:28; 15:4), so He will defeat Israel's enemies and snuff them out "like a wick" (Isa. 43:17 NIV).

When God forgives and restores His people, He wants them to forget the failures of the past, witness for Him in the present, and claim His promises for the future (vv. 18–21). Why should we remember that which God has forgotten? (v. 25) He forgave them, not because they brought Him sacrifices—for they had no altar in Babylon—but purely because of His mercy and grace.

God chose Israel and redeemed them, but He also formed them for Himself (44:1–20). In this chapter, Isaiah contrasts God's forming of Israel (vv. 1–8) and the Gentiles forming their own gods (vv. 9–20). "I have formed thee" is a special theme in chapters 43—44 (43:1, 7, 21; 44:2, 24). Because God formed them, chose them, and redeemed them, they had nothing to fear. He will pour water on the land and His Spirit on the people (59:21; Ezek. 34:26; Joel 2:28–29; John 7:37–39), and both will prosper to the glory of the Lord. The final fulfillment of this will be in the future kingdom age when the Messiah reigns.

Isaiah 44:9–20 shows the folly of idolatry and should be compared with Psalm 115. Those who defend idols and worship them are just like them: blind and ignorant and nothing. God made people in His own image, and now they are making gods in their own image! Part of the tree becomes a god, and the rest of the tree becomes fuel for the fire. The worshipper is "feeding on ashes" and deriving no benefit at all from the worship experience.

But God formed Israel (Isa. 44:21, 24), forgave His people their sins (v. 22; see 43:25), and is glorified in them (44:23). He speaks to His people and is faithful to keep His Word (v. 26). May we never take for granted the privilege we have of knowing and worshipping the true and living God!

**(3) God's Servant Messiah (Isa. 42).** Isaiah 42:1–7 is the first of four "Servant Songs" in Isaiah, referring to God's Servant, the Messiah. The others are 49:1–6; 50:1–11; and 52:13—53:12. Contrast "Behold, they [the idols] are all vanity" (41:29) with "Behold my servant" (42:1). Matthew 12:14–21 applies these words to the earthly ministry of Jesus Christ. He could have destroyed His enemies (the reed and flax), but He was patient and merciful. The Father delights in His Son (Matt. 3:17; 17:5).

It is through the ministry of the Servant that God will accomplish His great plan of salvation for this world. God chose Him, God upheld Him, and God enabled Him to succeed in His mission. Because of the death and resurrection of Jesus Christ, one day there will be a glorious kingdom, and God will "bring justice to the nations" (Isa. 42:1 NIV). Jesus Christ is "the light of the world" (John 8:12), and that includes the Gentiles (Isa. 42:6; Acts 13:47–48; Luke 1:79). Isaiah 42:7 refers to the nation's deliverance from Babylon (29:18; 32:3; 35:5) as well as to the sinner's deliverance from condemnation (61:1–3; Luke 4:18–19).

The closing section (Isa. 42:10–25) describes a singing nation (vv. 10–12), giving praise to the Lord, and a silent God who breaks that silence to become a shouting conqueror (vv. 13–17). God is longsuffering toward sinners, but when He begins to work, He wastes no time! The "servant" in verses 18–25 is the people of Israel, blind to their own sins and deaf to God's voice (6:9–10); yet the Lord graciously forgave them and led them out of bondage. Now God says to the Babylonians, "Send them back!" (42:22 NIV).

How sad it is when God disciplines us and we do not understand what He is doing or take it to heart (v. 25). Israel's captivity in Babylon cured the nation of their idolatry, but it did not create within them a desire to please God and glorify Him.

## 3. GOD IS GREATER THAN OUR ENEMIES (45:1—48:22)

These chapters deal with the overthrow of Babylon, and one of the major themes is, "I am the Lord, and there is none else" (45:5–6, 14, 18, 21–22; 46:9). Jehovah again reveals Himself as the true and living God in contrast to the dumb and dead idols.

**The conqueror described (45:1–25).** Just as prophets, priests, and kings were anointed for service, so Cyrus was anointed by God to perform his special service for Israel's sake. In this sense, Cyrus was a "messiah," an "anointed one." God called him by name over a century before he was born! Cyrus was the human instrument for the conquest, but it was Jehovah God who gave the victories. Anyone who opposed Cyrus was arguing with God, and that was like the clay commanding the potter or the child ordering his parents (vv. 9–10). God raised up Cyrus to do His specific will (v. 13), and nothing would prevent him from succeeding. Note the emphasis on salvation. The idols cannot save Babylon (v. 20), but God is the Savior of Israel (vv. 15, 17). He is "a just God and a Savior" (v. 21), and He offers salvation to the whole world (v. 22). It was this verse that brought the light of salvation to the great English pastor Charles Haddon Spurgeon when he was a youth seeking the Lord.

**The false gods disgraced (46:1–13).** Bel was the Babylonian sun god, and Nebo was his son, the god of writing and learning. But both of them together could not stop Cyrus! As the Babylonians fled from the enemy, they had to carry their gods, but their gods went into captivity with the prisoners of war! God assures His people that He will carry them from the womb to the tomb. Verse 4 is the basis for a stanza of the familiar song "How Firm a Foundation" that is usually omitted from our hymnals:

E'en down to old age, all My people shall prove,

My sovercign, eternal unchangeable love,

And then when grey hairs shall their temples adorn,

Like lambs they shall still in My bosom be borne.

—Richard Keen

How comforting it is to know that our God cares for us before we are born (Ps. 139:13–16), when we get old, and each moment in between!

**The city destroyed (47:1–15).** Babylon, the proud queen, is now a humbled slave. "I will continue forever—the eternal queen!" she boasted (v. 7 NIV). But in a moment, the judgment for her sins caught up with her; and she became a widow. Neither her idols nor her occult practices (vv. 12–14) were able to warn her or prepare her for her destruction. But God knew that Babylon would fall, because He planned it ages ago! He called

Cyrus, who swooped down on Babylon like a bird of prey. Babylon showed no mercy to the Jews, and God judged them accordingly.

**The Jewish remnant delivered (48:1–22).** The Jews had become comfortable and complacent in their captivity and did not want to leave. They had followed the counsel of Jeremiah (Jer. 29:4–7) and had houses, gardens, and families, but they had become so attached to those things that it would not be easy for them to pack up and go to the Holy Land. Nevertheless, the Holy Land was where they belonged and where God had a work for them to do. God told them that they were hypocritical in using His name and identifying with His city but not obeying His will (Isa. 48:1–2). They were stubborn (v. 4) and were not excited about the new things God was doing for them.

Had they obeyed the Lord in the first place, they would have experienced peace and not war (vv. 18–19), but it was not too late. He had put them into the furnace to refine them and prepare them for their future work (v. 10). "Go forth from Babylon! Flee from the Chaldeans!" was God's command (v. 20 NKJV; see Jer. 50:8; 51:6, 45; Rev. 18:4). God would go before them and prepare the way, and they had nothing to fear.

One would think that the Jews would have been eager to leave their "prison" and return to their land to see God do new and great things for them. But they had grown accustomed to the security of bondage and had forgotten the challenges of freedom. The church today can easily grow complacent with its comfort and affluence. God may have to put us into the furnace to remind us that we are here to be servants and not consumers or spectators.

# QUESTIONS FOR PERSONAL REFLECTION
# OR GROUP DISCUSSION

1. What verses or passages from Isaiah 40 could be given to someone in a crisis?

2. Isaiah 40:1–11 is often read in the season leading up to Christmas, and Matthew 3:1–5 quotes this passage in describing the ministry of John the Baptist. Why is 40:1–11 a suitable passage to describe the coming of Christ? How does it fit John the Baptist?

3. In Isaiah 40—48, what areas of life does Isaiah say God is greater than?

4. God told His people several times in Isaiah 41—44 to "fear not." Why shouldn't they be afraid?

5. How does God's sovereignty over the unconverted give hope to believers?

6. What hope can a believer have about his or her past (Isa. 43:25)?

7. In what ways can the Messiah give someone a future hope (see Isa. 42:1–7)?

8. For today, what hope can we find in Isaiah 43:1–7?

9. What are some appropriate ways to respond to the greatness of God?

10. In what ways can believers bring encouragement to each other in times of struggle?

# Chapter Ten

# THIS IS GOD'S SERVANT

## (Isaiah 49:1—52:12)

A plaque in a friend's office reads, "The world is full of people who want to serve in an advisory capacity."

But Jesus Christ did not come with good advice: He came with good news, the good news that sinners can be forgiven and life can become excitingly new. The gospel is good news to us, but it was "bad news" to the Son of God; for it meant that He would need to come to earth in human form and die on a cross as the sacrifice for the sins of the world.

These chapters present God's Servant, Messiah, in three important relationships: to the Gentile nations (49:1—50:3), to His Father (50:4–11), and to His people Israel (51:1—52:12).

## 1. THE SERVANT AND THE GENTILES (49:1—50:3)

The Servant addresses the nations that did not know Israel's God. The Gentiles were "far off," and only God's Servant could bring them near (Eph. 2:11–22). Christ confirmed God's promises to the Jews and also extended God's grace to the Gentiles (Rom. 15:8–12). In this message, God's Servant explains His ministry as bringing light in the darkness (Isa. 49:1–7), liberty to the captive (vv. 8–13), and love and hope to the discouraged (49:14—50:3).

**Light in the darkness (49:1–7).** What right did God's Servant have to address the Gentile nations with such authority? From before His birth, He was called by God to His ministry (Jer. 1:5; Gal. 1:15), and God prepared Him like a sharp sword and a polished arrow (Heb. 4:12; Rev. 1:16). Messiah came as both a Servant and a Warrior, serving those who trust Him and ultimately judging those who resist Him.

All of God's servants should be like prepared weapons. "It is not great talents God blesses so much as great likeness to Jesus," wrote Robert Murray McCheyne. "A holy minister [servant] is an awful weapon in the hand of God."

The Jewish nation was called to glorify God and be a light to the Gentiles, but they failed in their mission. This is why Messiah is called "Israel" in Isaiah 49:3: He did the work that Israel was supposed to do. Today, the church is God's light in the dark world (Acts 13:46–49; Matt. 5:14–16), and like Israel, we seem to be failing in our mission to take the good news to the ends of the earth. We cannot do the job very effectively when only five percent of the average local church budget is devoted to evangelism!

As Jesus Christ ministered on earth, especially to His own people Israel, there were times when His work seemed in vain (Isa. 49:4). The religious leaders opposed Him, the disciples did not always understand Him, and those He helped did not always thank Him. He lived and labored by faith, and God gave Him success.

Our Lord could not minister to the Gentiles until first He ministered to the Jews (vv. 5–6). Read carefully Matthew 10:5–6; 15:24; Luke 24:44–49; Acts 3:25–26; 13:46–47; and Romans 1:16. When our Lord returned to heaven, He left behind a believing remnant of Jews who carried on His work. We must never forget that "salvation is of the Jews" (John 4:22). The Bible is a Jewish book, the first believers and missionaries were Jews, and the Gentiles would not have heard the gospel had it not been brought to them by Jews. Messiah was despised by both Jews and Gentiles (Isa. 49:7), but He did God's work and was glorified (Phil. 2:1–11).

**Liberty to the captives (49:8–13).** Not only is God's Servant the "new Israel," but He is also the "new Moses" in setting His people free. Jesus Christ is God's covenant (42:6), so we can be sure that God will keep His promises. Moses led the nation out of bondage in Egypt, and God will lead His people out of captivity in Babylon. Joshua led the people into their land so they could claim their inheritance, and God will bring them back to their land "to reassign its desolate inheritances" (49:8 NIV).

How does this apply to the Gentiles? If God had not restored the people, the city, and the temple, He could not have fulfilled His promises concerning the Messiah. Had there been no Bethlehem, where would He have been born? Had there been no Nazareth, where would He have grown up? Had there been no Jerusalem and no temple, where would He have taught, suffered, and died? And He did this for the Gentiles as well as for the Jews.

Verses 10–12 look beyond the deliverance from Babylon in 536 BC toward the future glorious kingdom. The Lord will call the Jewish people from the ends of the earth and gather them again in their land (Isa. 14:1–3l; 35:6; 40:11; 43:19).

**Love and hope to the discouraged (49:14—50:3).** "The LORD comforts his people and will have compassion on his afflicted ones" (49:13 NIV). So sing the people of God as they contemplate their future deliverance, but the people of the captivity and those left in "the desolate inheritances" are not so happy. Instead of singing, they are complaining: "The LORD has forsaken me, and my Lord has forgotten me" (v. 14 NKJV).

The Lord assures them of His love by comparing Himself to a compassionate mother (vv. 14–23), a courageous warrior (vv. 24–26), and a constant lover (50:1–3).

*A compassionate mother (49:14–23).* The Bible emphasizes the fatherhood of God, but there is also a "motherhood" side to God's nature that we must not forget. God is compassionate and comforts us as a mother comforts her children (66:13). Isaiah pictures Israel as a nursing child, totally dependent on the Lord, who will never forget them or forsake them. The high priest bore the names of the tribes of Israel on his shoulders and over his heart (Ex. 28:6–9), engraved on jewels, but God has engraved His children's names on His hands. The word *engraved* means "to cut into," signifying its permanence. God can never forget Zion or Zion's children.

Zion seems like a forsaken and barren mother, but she will be so blessed of God that there will be no room for her children! They will be like beautiful bridal ornaments, not decrepit refugees from captivity. Once again, the prophet looked ahead to the end of the age when the Gentiles will honor Jehovah and Israel, and kings and queens will be babysitters for Israel's children!

*A courageous warrior (49:24–26).* The Babylonians were fierce warriors, but the Lord would snatch Israel from their grasp. In His compassion, He would set the captives free and see to it that Babylon would never afflict them again. The fact that God permitted Babylon to conquer His people did not mean that God was weak or unconcerned. When the right time comes, He will set His people free: "they shall not be ashamed that wait for me" (v. 23).

*A constant lover (50:1–3).* The image of Israel as the wife of Jehovah is found often in the prophets (54:4–5; 62:1–5; Jer. 2:1–3; 3:1–11; Hos. 2; Ezek. 16). Israel was "married" to Jehovah when they accepted the covenant at Sinai (Ex. 19—20), but they violated that covenant by "playing the harlot" and worshipping idols. But God did not forsake His people even though they had been unfaithful to Him.

The Mosaic permission for divorce is found in Deuteronomy 24:1–4 (see Matt. 19:1–12). The "certificate of divorce" declared that the former marriage was broken and that the woman was free to remarry. But it also prevented the woman from returning to her former husband. God had indeed "divorced" the northern kingdom and allowed it to be assimilated by the Assyrians (Jer. 3:8), so she could not return. But He had not "divorced" the southern kingdom; He had only permitted His unfaithful wife to suffer chastening at the hands of Babylon. He would forgive her and receive her back again.

The second picture in this paragraph is that of a poor family selling their children into servitude (2 Kings 4:1–7; Neh. 5:1–5). God had not sold His people; by their sins, they had sold themselves. God had called to them many times and tried to turn them back from their wicked ways, but they had refused to listen. Judah did not go into exile because of God's weakness, but because of their own sinfulness.

How could the people say they were forgotten and forsaken, when the Lord is a compassionate mother, a courageous warrior, and a constant lover? He is faithful to His Word even when we are unfaithful (2 Tim. 2:11–13). He is faithful to chasten when we rebel (Heb. 12:1–11), but He is also faithful to forgive when we repent and confess (1 John 1:9).

The Servant's message to the Gentiles was one of hope and blessing. He would deal with His people so that they, in turn, could bring God's blessing to the Gentiles.

## 2. THE SERVANT AND THE LORD GOD (50:4–11)

In the first two "Servant Songs" (42:1–7; 49:1–7), you find hints of opposition to Messiah's ministry, but in this third song, His suffering is vividly described. When we get to the fourth song (52:12—53:12), we will be told not only how He suffered, but why His suffering is necessary.

Note that four times in this passage the Servant uses the name "Lord God." "Jehovah Adonai" can be translated "Sovereign Lord," and you will find this title nowhere else in the "Servant Songs." According to Robert B. Girdlestone, the name "Jehovah Adonai" means that "God is the owner of each member of the human family, and that He consequently claims the unrestricted obedience of all" (*Synonyms of the Old Testament*, Eerdmans, 1951, 34). So the emphasis here is on the Servant's submission to the Lord God in every area of His life and service.

His mind was submitted to the Lord God so that He could learn His work and His will (50:4). Everything Jesus said and did was taught to Him by His Father (John 5:19, 30; 6:38; 8:28). He prayed to the Father for guidance (John 11:42; Mark 1:35) and meditated on the Word. What God taught the Servant, the Servant shared with those who needed encouragement and help. The Servant sets a good example here for all who know the importance of a daily "quiet time" with the Lord.

The Servant's will was also yielded to the Lord God. An "opened ear" is one that hears and obeys the voice of the master. The people to whom Isaiah ministered were neither "willing" nor "obedient" (Isa. 1:19), but the Servant did gladly the will of the Lord God. This was not easy, for it meant yielding His body to wicked men who mocked Him, whipped Him, spat on Him, and then nailed Him to a cross (Matt. 26:67; 27:26, 30).

The Servant did all of this by faith in the Lord God (Isa. 50:7–11). He was determined to do God's will even if it meant going to a cross (Luke 9:51; John 18:1–11), for He knew that the Lord God would help Him. The Servant was falsely accused, but He knew that God would vindicate Him and eventually put His enemies to shame. Keep in mind that when Jesus Christ was ministering here on earth, He had to live by faith even as we must today. He did not use His divine powers selfishly for Himself but trusted God and depended on the power of the Spirit.

Verses 10–11 are addressed especially to the Jewish remnant, but they have an application to God's people today. His faithful ones were perplexed at what God was doing, but He assured them that their faith would not go unrewarded. Dr. Bob Jones, Sr. often said, "Never doubt in the dark what God has told you in the light." But the unbelieving ones who try to eliminate the darkness by lighting their own fires (i.e., following their own schemes) will end up in sorrow and suffering. In obedience to the Lord, you may find yourself in the darkness, but do not panic, for He will bring you the light you need just at the right time.

## 3. THE SERVANT AND ISRAEL (51:1—52:12)

This section contains several admonitions: "hearken to me" (51:1; also 4, 7); "awake, awake" (vv. 9, 17; 52:1–6); and "depart, depart" (vv. 7–12). Except for 51:9–16, which is a prayer addressed to the Lord, each of these admonitions is from God to His people in Babylon.

**"Hearken to me" (51:1–8).** These three admonitions are addressed to the faithful remnant in Israel, the people described in 50:10. In the first admonition (51:1–3), the Lord told them to look back and remember Abraham and Sarah, the progenitors of the Jewish nation (Gen. 12—25). God called them "alone," but from these two elderly people came a nation as numerous as the dust of the earth and the stars of the heaven (13:16; 15:5). The remnant leaving Babylon was small and weak, but God was able to increase them into a mighty nation and also turn their ravaged land into a paradise. "Be comforted!" God said to His people. "The best is yet to come!"

In the second command (Isa. 51:4–6), God told them to look ahead and realize that justice would come to the world and they would be vindicated by the Lord. Note the emphasis on the word *my*: My people, My nation, My justice, My righteousness, My arms, and My salvation. This is the grace of God, doing for His people what they did not deserve and what they could not do for themselves. The "arm of the Lord" is a key concept in Isaiah's prophecies (30:30; 40:10; 51:5, 9; 52:10; 53:1; 59:16; 62:8; 63:5, 12). Heaven and earth will pass away, but God's righteousness and salvation will last forever. That righteousness will be displayed in a special way when Messiah returns and establishes His kingdom on earth.

The third admonition (51:7–8) focuses on looking within, where we find either fear or faith. Why should the nation fear men when God is on its side? "Behold, God is my salvation, I will trust and not be afraid" (Isa. 12:2 NKJV). "Sanctify the LORD of hosts himself; and let him be your fear, and let him be your dread" (8:13). To have God's law in your heart means to belong to Him and be saved (Jer. 31:31–34; Heb. 10:16). The moth and the worm shall destroy the enemy, but God's salvation will endure. Moths and worms do not do their work conspicuously, but they work efficiently just the same. The seeds of destruction were already in the Babylonian Empire, and the leaders did not know it.

**"Awake, awake" (51:9—52:6).** "Hearken to me" was spoken to admonish the people, but "awake, awake" is for the rousing of the Lord (51:9–16) and of Jerusalem (vv. 17–23; 52:1–6).

The remnant in Babylon prayed as though God were asleep and needed to be awakened (Ps. 7:6; 44:23; 78:65–72). They wanted God to bare His arm as He did when He defeated Pharaoh and redeemed His people from Egyptian bondage. The return from Babylon was looked upon as another "exodus" (Isa. 43:16–17; 49:9–12), with God wholly in charge and the enemy completely defeated.

God replied to their prayer with words of comfort (51:12–16; see vv. 3, 19). He reminded them again of the frailty of man (see 40:6–8) and the power of God the Creator (51:13). Why should they be afraid of grass when the God of the universe was on their side? Because they are His people, with whom He has deposited His Word, He will release them, protect them, and provide for them. They had an important task to perform and He would enable them to do it.

In the second "wake-up call," the prophet spoke to the ruined city of Jerusalem (vv. 17–23) and pictured her as a mother in a drunken stupor with no children to help her. In the Bible, judgment is sometimes pictured as the drinking of a cup of wine (29:9; 63:6; Ps. 75:8; Jer. 25:15–16; Rev. 14:10). Jerusalem's children had gone into captivity, but now they would return and give their "mother" new hope and a new beginning. God will take the cup of judgment from the Jews and give it to their enemies. To put your foot on the neck of your enemies was a humiliating declaration of their defeat, but instead of Babylon "walking on" the Jews, the Jews would "walk on" the Babylonians!

The third "wake-up call" (Isa. 52:1–6) is also addressed to Jerusalem and is a command not only to wake up but to dress up! It is not enough for her to put off her stupor (51:17–23); she must also put on her glorious garments. Babylon the "queen" would fall to the dust in shame (47:1), but Jerusalem would rise up from the dust and be enthroned as a queen! Egypt had enslaved God's people, Assyria had oppressed them, and Babylon had taken them captive, but now that was ended. Of course, the ultimate fulfillment of this promise will occur when the Messiah returns, delivers Jerusalem from her enemies, and establishes Mount Zion as the joy of all the earth (61:4–11).

The city of Jerusalem is called "the Holy City" eight times in Scripture (Neh. 11:1, 18; Isa. 48:2; 52:1; Dan. 9:24; Matt. 4:5; 27:53; Rev. 11:2). It has been "set apart" by God for His exclusive purposes, but when His people refused to obey Him, He ordered it destroyed, first by the Babylonians and then by the Romans.

During the captivity, God's name was blasphemed because the enemy taunted the Jews and asked them why their great God did not deliver them (Ps. 115; 137). Paul quoted Isaiah 52:5 in Romans 2:24. But when the remnant is restored, they will know God's name and seek to honor it.

**"Depart, depart" (52:7–12).** The defeat of Babylon by Cyrus was certainly good news to the Jews because it meant freedom for the captives (40:9; 41:27). The good news we share today is that Jesus Christ can set the prisoners free (Rom. 10:15). For decades, the remnant had suffered in a foreign country, without an altar or a priesthood, but now they would return to their land, rebuild their temple, and restore their God-given ministry.

It has well been said that "good news is for sharing," and that is what happens in Jerusalem. The leaders (watchmen) take up the message and sing together to the glory of God (Isa. 44:23). But they not only hear what God has done; they also see it happening! The wilderness will join the song because the desolate cities and "waste places" will be transformed (51:3). The remnant prayed for God's holy arm to work, and He answered their prayer (v. 9).

Isaiah liked to use repetition: "Comfort ye, comfort ye" (40:1); "awake,

awake" (51:9, 17; 52:1); and now, "depart, depart" (52:11). It seems strange that God would have to urge His people to leave a place of captivity, but some of them had grown accustomed to Babylon and were reluctant to leave. The first group, about fifty thousand people, left Babylon in 539–538 BC when Cyrus issued his decree. They were under the leadership of Sheshbazzar, Zerubbabel, and Jeshua the high priest (Ezra 1—2). They carried with them "the vessels of the Lord" (Isa. 52:11), the articles that were needed for the service in the temple. A second group of nearly eighteen hundred people led by Ezra left in 458 BC.

God commanded them to depart because Babylon was a condemned city (Jer. 50:8ff.; 51:6, 45). He warned them not to linger but to get out quickly while they had the opportunity (Isa. 48:20). They did not have to flee like criminals, but there was no reason to tarry. He also cautioned them not to take any of Babylon's uncleanness with them. "Touch no unclean thing" (52:11) would certainly include the whole Babylonian system of idolatry and occult practices that had helped to ruin the Jewish nation (47:11–15). Paul made the application to believers today in 2 Corinthians 6:14—7:1.

God had a special word for the priests and Levites who were carrying the vessels of the temple: "Come out from it [Babylon] and be pure" (Isa. 52:11 NIV). This is a good command for all of God's servants to obey. If we defile ourselves, we will also defile the work of the Lord. How tragic for a holy ministry to be a source of defilement to God's people!

The prophet added a final word of encouragement: "The LORD will go before you; and the God of Israel will be your reward" (v. 12; see 58:8). This reminds us of Israel's exodus from Egypt when the Lord went before them (Ex. 13:21) and stood between them and the enemy (14:19–20). When God's people obey God's will, they can always count on God's leading and protection.

Isaiah has prepared the way for the "heart" of God's revelation of the Servant Messiah, the fourth Servant Song (52:13—53:12). We must prepare our hearts, for we are walking on holy ground.

# QUESTIONS FOR PERSONAL REFLECTION
# OR GROUP DISCUSSION

1. How did God's people view the Messiah's mission (see Isa. 49:5–6a)?

2. How did God expand His people's understanding of the mission (see Isa. 49:6b)? How might His people have felt about this expansion?

3. How will God use His people to accomplish His mission (see Isa. 49:8–13)?

4. If you had received the message of Isaiah 49:1—50:3 as an exile in Babylon, what comfort from this passage would you have underlined in your scroll?

5. Why do you think the Jews originally failed to accomplish their God-given mission to be light for the Gentiles? Can we blame them? Please explain.

6. Read Ephesians 2:11–22 and Romans 15:8–21. How did Christ bring the Gentiles near?

7. What do you think caused "the wall" between the Jews and Gentiles (see Eph. 2:14)?

8. As a Gentile hearing this news from Paul, how do you think you would have responded?

9. How does the Messiah's relationship to the Father demonstrate a servant's attitude of mind (Isa. 50:4), of will (Isa. 50:5), and of body (Isa. 50:6)?

10. In order to become a model disciple in mind, will, and body, what goals reflecting servant attitude and activities would you set for yourself?

# Chapter Eleven

# CLIMBING MOUNT EVEREST

## (Isaiah 52:13—53:12)

T hese five matchless stanzas of the fourth Servant poem are the Mount Everest of messianic prophecy." So wrote Old Testament scholar Dr. Kyle M. Yates over fifty years ago, and his words still stand. This passage is at the heart of chapters 49—57, and its message is at the heart of the gospel. Like Mount Everest, Isaiah 53 stands out in beauty and grandeur, but only because it reveals Jesus Christ and takes us to Mount Calvary.

The messianic interpretation of Isaiah 53 was held by Jewish rabbis till the twelfth century. After that, Jewish scholars started interpreting the passage as a description of the sufferings of the nation of Israel. But how could Israel die for the sins of Israel (v. 8)? And who declared that Israel was innocent of sin and therefore had suffered unjustly (v. 9)? No, the prophet wrote about an innocent individual, not a guilty nation. He made it crystal clear that this individual died for the sins of the guilty so that the guilty might go free.

The Servant that Isaiah describes is the Messiah, and the New Testament affirms that this Servant-Messiah is Jesus of Nazareth, the Son of God (Matt. 8:17; Mark 15:28; Luke 22:37; John 12:38; Acts 8:27–40; 1 Peter 2:21–24). Isaiah 53 is quoted or alluded to in the New Testament

more frequently than any other Old Testament chapter. The index of quo-
tations in the appendix of my Greek New Testament gives at least forty-
one different citations, and this may not be all of them.

The fifteen verses that comprise the fourth Servant Song fall into five
stanzas of three verses each, and each of these stanzas reveals an important
truth about the Servant and what He accomplished for us.

## 1. EXALTATION: THE SHOCKING SERVANT (52:13–15)

His people did not admire or desire the Servant (52:2–3), and yet when it
was all over, He shocked and astonished kings! If we take these verses in
their chronological order, we see that people were shocked by His appearance (52:14), His exaltation (v. 13), and His message (v. 15). We have here
our Lord's suffering and death, His resurrection and ascension, and the
worldwide proclamation of the gospel.

**Startled at the Servant's appearance (v. 14).** "They shall see My
Servant beaten and bloodied, so disfigured one would scarcely know it was
a person standing there" (TLB). "So disfigured did He look that He seemed
no longer human" (JB). When you consider all that Jesus endured physi-
cally between the time of His arrest and His crucifixion, it is no wonder
He no longer looked like a man. Not only were His legal rights taken away
from Him, including the right to a fair trial, but His human rights were
taken from Him, so that He was not even treated like a person, let alone a
Jewish citizen.

When He was questioned before Annas, Jesus was slapped by an officer
(John 18:22). At the hearing before Caiaphas, He was spat upon, slapped,
and beaten on the head with fists (Matt. 26:67; Mark 14:65; Luke 22:63).
Pilate scourged Him (John 19:1; Matt 27:26; Mark 15:15), and his soldiers
beat Him (John 19:3). Scourging was so terrible that prisoners were known
to die from the ordeal. "I gave my back to the smiters," said God's Servant,
"and my cheeks to them that plucked off the hair: I hid not my face from

shame and spitting" (Isa. 50:6). And they were doing this to the very Son of God!

The graphic account of His suffering that is given in some sermons is not found in Scripture, except perhaps in Psalm 22. The gospel writers give us the facts but not the details. Suffice it to say that when the sinners were finished with the Savior, He did not look human, and people were so appalled they turned their faces away. What was done to Jesus should have been done to Barabbas—and to us.

*Isa 52*

**Startled at the Servant's exaltation (v. 13).** The Servant suffered and died, but He did not remain dead. He was "exalted and extolled, and [made] very high." The phrase deal *prudently* means "to be successful in one's endeavor." What looked to men like a humiliating defeat was in the eyes of God a great victory (Col. 2:15). "I have glorified thee on the earth," He told His Father; "I have finished the work which thou gavest me to do" (John 17:4).

Jesus was not only raised from the dead, but His body was glorified. He ascended to heaven, where He sat at the right hand of the Father. He has all authority (Matt. 28:18) because all things have been put under His feet (Eph. 1:20–23). There is no one in the universe higher than Jesus. What an astonishment to those who esteemed Him the lowest of the low (see Phil. 2:1–11)!

**Startled at the Servant's message (v. 15).** The people whose mouths dropped open with astonishment at His humiliation and exaltation will shut their mouths in guilt when they hear His proclamation. Paul interpreted this as the preaching of the gospel to the Gentile nations (Rom. 15:20–21). "That every mouth may be stopped, and all the world may become guilty before God" (3:19).

Many people have been tortured and killed in an inhumane way, but knowing about their suffering does not touch our conscience, though it may arouse our sympathy. Our Lord's sufferings and death were different, because they involved everybody in the world. The gospel message is not "Christ died," for that is only a fact in history, like "Napoleon died." The gospel message is that "Christ died *for our sins*" (1 Cor. 15:1–4, italics mine). You and I are as guilty of Christ's death as Annas, Caiaphas, Herod Antipas, and Pilate.

Now we see why people are astonished when they understand the message of the gospel: This Man whom they condemned has declared that they are condemned unless they turn from sin and trust Him. You cannot rejoice in the good news of salvation until first you face the bad news of condemnation. Jesus did not suffer and die because He was guilty, but because we were guilty. People are astonished at this fact; it shuts their mouths.

The word translated "sprinkle" in Isaiah 52:15 can be translated "startle," but most likely it refers to the ceremonial cleansing that was an important part of the Mosaic sacrificial system (Lev. 14:1–7, 16; 16:14–15; Num. 8:7). While the sprinkling of blood, water, and oil did not take away sins, it did make the recipient ceremonially clean and accepted before God. Because of the sacrifice of Christ, we can tell all the nations that forgiveness and redemption are offered free to all who will receive Him (1 Peter. 1:1–2).

## 2. HUMILIATION: THE SORROWING SERVANT (53:1–3)

Isaiah 53 describes the life and ministry of Jesus Christ (vv. 1–4), His death (vv. 5–8) and burial (v. 9), and His resurrection and exaltation (vv. 10–12). The theme that ties the chapter together is that the innocent Servant died in the place of the guilty. When theologians speak about "the vicarious atonement," that is what they mean. We cannot explain everything about the cross, but this much seems clear: Jesus took the place of guilty sinners and paid the price for their salvation.

There is quite a contrast between "the arm of the Lord," which speaks of mighty power, and "a root out of a dry ground," which is an image of humiliation and weakness. When God made the universe, He used His fingers (Ps. 8:3), and when He delivered Israel from Egypt, it was by His strong hand (Ex. 13:3). But to save lost sinners, He had to bare His mighty arm! Yet people still refuse to believe this great demonstration of God's power (Rom. 1:16; John 12:37–40).

The Servant is God, and yet He becomes human and grows up! The Child is born—that is His humanity; the Son is given—that is His deity (Isa. 9:6). In writing about Israel's future, Isaiah has already used the image of a tree: The Messiah is the Branch of the Lord (4:2); the remnant is like the stumps of trees chopped down (6:13); the proud nations will be hewn down like trees, but out of David's seemingly dead stump, the "rod of Jesse" will come (10:33—11:1). Because Jesus Christ is God, He is the "root of David," but because He is man, He is the "offspring of David" (Rev. 22:16).

Israel was not a paradise when Jesus was born; politically and spiritually, it was a wilderness of dry ground. He did not come as a great tree but as a "tender plant." He was born in poverty in Bethlehem and grew up in a carpenter's shop in despised Nazareth (John 1:43–46). Because of His words and works, Jesus attracted great crowds, but nothing about His physical appearance made Him different from any other Jewish man. While few people deliberately try to be unattractive, modern society has made a religion out physical beauty. It is good to remember that Jesus succeeded without it.

Once they understood what He demanded of them, how did most people treat the Servant? The way they treated any other slave: They despised Him, put a cheap price on Him (thirty pieces of silver), and "looked the other way when He went by" (Isa. 53:3 TLB). They were ashamed of Him because He did not represent the things that were important to them: things like wealth (Luke 16:14), social prestige (14:7–14; 15:12), reputation (18:9–14), being served by others (22:24–27), and pampering yourself (Matt. 16:21–28). He is rejected today for the same reasons.

### 3. EXPIATION: THE SMITTEN SERVANT (53:4–6)

This is the heart of the passage, and it presents the heart of the gospel message: the innocent Servant dying as the sacrifice for sin. This message was at the heart of Israel's religious system—the innocent animal sacrifice dying for the guilty sinner (Lev. 16).

Jesus bore our sins on the cross (1 Peter 2:24), but He also identified with the consequences of Adam's sin when He ministered to needy people. Matthew 8:14–17 applies Isaiah 53:4 to our Lord's healing ministry and not to His atoning death. Every blessing we have in the Christian life comes because of the cross, but this verse does not teach that there is "healing in the atonement" and that every believer therefore has the "right" to be healed. The prophecy was fulfilled during our Lord's life, not His death.

The emphasis in verses 4–6 is on the plural pronouns: our griefs and sorrows, our iniquities, our transgressions. We have gone astray, we have turned to our own way. He did not die because of anything He had done, but because of what we had done.

He was "wounded," which means "pierced through." His hands and feet were pierced by nails (Ps. 22:16; Luke 24:39–40) and His side by a spear (John 19:31–37; Zech. 12:10; Rev. 1:7). He was crucified, which was not a Jewish form of execution (John 12:32–33; 18:31–32). Capital punishment to the Jews meant stoning (Lev. 24:14; Num. 15:35–36). If they wanted to further humiliate the victim, they could publicly expose the corpse (Deut. 21:22–23), a practice that Peter related to the crucifixion (Acts 5:30; 10:39; 1 Peter 2:24).

On the cross, Jesus Christ was "bruised," which means "crushed under the weight of a burden." What was the burden? "The Lord hath laid on him the iniquity of us all" (Isa. 53:6; see v. 12; 1:4). Sin is indeed a burden that grows heavier the longer we resist God (Ps. 38:4).

He was "chastised" and given many "stripes," and yet that punishment brought us peace and healing. The only way a lawbreaker can be at peace with the law is to suffer the punishment that the law demands. Jesus kept the law perfectly, yet He suffered the whipping that belonged to us. Because He took our place, we now have peace with God and cannot be condemned by God's law (Rom. 5:1; 8:1). The "healing" in Isaiah 53:5 refers to the forgiveness of sins, not the healing of the body (1 Peter 2:24; Ps. 103:3). Sin is not only like a burden, but it is also like a sickness that only God can cure (Isa. 1:4–6; Jer. 30:12; Nah. 3:19).

Sin is serious. The prophet calls it transgression, which means rebellion against God, daring to cross the line that God has drawn (Isa. 53:5, 8). He also calls it iniquity, which refers to the crookedness of our sinful nature (vv. 5–6). In other words, we are sinners by choice and by nature. Like sheep, we are born with a nature that prompts us to go astray and like sheep we foolishly decide to go our own way. By nature we are born children of wrath (Eph. 2:3) and by choice we become children of disobedience (2:2). Under the law of Moses, the sheep died for the shepherd; but under grace, the Good Shepherd died for the sheep (John 10:1–18).

## 4. RESIGNATION: THE SILENT SERVANT (53:7–9)

A servant is not permitted to talk back; he or she must submit to the will of the master or mistress. Jesus Christ was silent before those who accused Him as well as those who afflicted Him. He was silent before Caiaphas (Matt. 26:62–63), the chief priests and elders (27:12), Pilate (27:14; John 19:9) and Herod Antipas (Luke 23:9). He did not speak when the soldiers mocked Him and beat Him (1 Peter 2:21–23). This is what impressed the Ethiopian treasurer as he read this passage in Isaiah (Acts 8:26–40).

Isaiah 53:7 speaks of His silence under suffering and verse 8 of His silence when illegally tried and condemned to death. In today's courts, a person can be found guilty of terrible crimes, but if it can be proved that something in the trial was illegal, the case must be tried again. Everything about His trials was illegal, yet Jesus did not appeal for another trial. "The cup which my Father hath given me, shall I not drink it?" (John 18:11).

The Servant is compared to a lamb (Isa. 53:7), which is one of the frequent symbols of the Savior in Scripture. A lamb died for each Jewish household at Passover (Ex. 12:1–13), and the Servant died for His people, the nation of Israel (Isa. 53:8). Jesus is "the Lamb of God who takes away the sin of the world" (John 1:29 NKJV), and twenty-eight times in the book of Revelation, Jesus Christ is referred to as the Lamb.

Since Jesus Christ was crucified with criminals as a criminal, it was logical that His dead body would be left unburied, but God had other plans. The burial of Jesus Christ is as much a part of the gospel as is His death (1 Cor. 15:1–5), for the burial is proof that He actually died. The Roman authorities would not have released the body to Joseph and Nicodemus if the victim had not been dead (John 19:38–42; Mark 15:42–47). A wealthy man like Joseph would never carve out a tomb for himself so near to a place of execution, particularly when his home was miles away. He prepared it for Jesus and had the spices and graveclothes ready for the burial. How wonderfully God fulfilled Isaiah's prophecy!

## 5. VINDICATION: THE SATISFIED SERVANT (53:10–12)

The prophet now explains the cross from God's point of view. Even though Jesus was crucified by the hands of wicked men, His death was determined beforehand by God (Act 2:22–23). Jesus was not a martyr, nor was His death an accident. He was God's sacrifice for the sins of the world.

He did not remain dead! "He shall prolong his days" (Isa. 53:10) means that the Servant was resurrected to live forever. In His resurrection, He triumphed over every enemy and claimed the spoils of victory (Eph. 1:19–23; 4:8). Satan offered Christ a glorious kingdom in return for worship (Matt. 4:8–10), which would have meant bypassing the cross. Jesus was "obedient unto death," and God "highly exalted him" (Phil. 2:8–10).

Another part of His "reward" is found in the statement "He shall see his seed [descendants]" (Isa. 53:10). To die childless was a grief and shame to the Jews, but Jesus gave birth to a spiritual family because of His travail on the cross (v. 11). Isaiah's statement about Isaiah's natural family (8:18) is quoted in Hebrews 2:13 and applied to Christ and His spiritual family.

The Servant's work on the cross brought satisfaction (Isa. 53:11). To begin with, the Servant satisfied the heart of the Father. "I do always those things that please him [the Father]" (John 8:29). The heavenly Father did not find enjoyment in seeing His beloved Son suffer, for the Father is not pleased with the death of the wicked, let alone the death of the righteous Son of God. But the Father was pleased that His Son's obedience accomplished the redemption that He had planned from eternity (1 Peter 1:20). "It is finished" (John 19:30).

The death of the Servant also satisfied the law of God. The theological term for this is "propitiation" (Rom. 3:25; 1 John 2:2). In pagan religions, the word meant "to offer a sacrifice to placate an angry god," but the Christian meaning is much richer. God is angry at sin because it offends His holiness and violates His holy law. In His holiness, He must judge sinners, but in His love, He desires to forgive them. God cannot ignore sin or compromise with it, for that would be contrary to His own nature and law.

How did God solve the problem? The Judge took the place of the criminals and met the just demands of His own holy law! "He was numbered with the transgressors" and even prayed for them (Isa. 53:12; Luke 22:37; 23:33–34). The law has been satisfied, and God can now graciously forgive all who receive His Son.

Grace is love that has paid a price, and sinners are saved by grace (Eph. 2:8–10). Justice can only condemn the wicked and justify the righteous (1 Kings 8:32), but grace justifies the ungodly when they trust Jesus Christ (see Isa. 53:11; Rom. 4:5)! To justify means "to declare righteous." He took our sins that we might receive the gift of His righteousness (2 Cor. 5:21; Rom. 5:17). Justification means God declares believing sinners righteous in Christ and never again keeps a record of their sins (see Ps. 32:1–2; Rom. 4:1–8).

On the morning of May 29, 1953, Sir Edmund Hillary and Tenzing Norgay conquered Mount Everest, the highest mountain peak in the world. Nobody has yet "conquered" Isaiah 53, for there are always new heights to reach. The important thing is to know personally God's righteous Servant, Jesus Christ, whose conquest of sin is the subject of this chapter. "By his knowledge [i.e., knowing Him personally by faith] shall my righteous servant justify many" (v. 11).

"Now this is eternal life: that they may know you, the only true God, and Jesus Christ, whom you have sent" (John 17:3 NIV).

# QUESTIONS FOR PERSONAL REFLECTION
# OR GROUP DISCUSSION

1. What important truths do each of the five stanzas of Isaiah 52:13—53:12 reveal?

2. How do the sufferings and death of Jesus differ from that of other people?

3. Why was Jesus rejected and shamed by the Jews?

4. Should we blame modern Jews for this? Please explain.

5. How does Isaiah 53:4–6 explain the heart of the gospel message?

6. Why is Jesus often referred to as a lamb? Where else in the Bible do you find this lamb imagery?

7. In what way did Christ's death on the cross bring satisfaction?

8.  Contrast justice with grace.


9.  What is justification? Who is justified before God?

# Chapter Twelve

# PROMISES AND PUNISHMENTS

## (Isaiah 54—59)

T he Servant obediently finished His work on earth, and today He is at work in heaven, interceding for God's people (Heb. 7:25; Rom. 8:34). But what are the consequences of His sacrifice? What difference does it make that He endured all that suffering? To Israel, it means restoration (Isa. 54:1–17); to the Gentile nations, it means an invitation (55:1—56:8); and to rebellious sinners, it means an accusation (56:9—59:21), a warning from the Lord that they need to repent.

## RESTORATION FOR ISRAEL (54:1–17)

The image in this chapter is that of Jehovah, the faithful husband, forgiving Israel, the unfaithful wife, and restoring her to the place of blessing. Isaiah has used the marriage image before (50:1–3) and will use it again (62:4). Jeremiah also used it (Jer. 3:8), and it is an important theme in both Hosea (chap. 2) and Ezekiel (chaps. 16 and 23). The nation was "married" to Jehovah at Mount Sinai, but she committed adultery by turning to other gods, and the Lord had to abandon her temporarily. However, the prophets promise that Israel will be restored when Messiah comes and establishes His kingdom.

What kind of restoration will it be? For one thing, it is a restoration to joy and therefore an occasion for singing (Isa. 54:1). Isaiah is certainly the prophet of song; he mentioned songs and singing more than thirty times in his book. The immediate occasion for this joy is the nation's deliverance from captivity, but the ultimate fulfillment is when the Redeemer comes to Zion and the nation is born anew (59:20).

It will also be a restoration to fruitfulness when the nation will increase and need more space (54:1–3). The nation had been diminished because of the Babylonian invasion, but God would help them multiply again. At the end of this age, only a believing remnant will enter into the kingdom, but the Lord will enlarge the nation abundantly. Israel may feel like a barren woman, unable to have children, but she will increase to the glory of God. God will do for her what He did for Sarah and Abraham (49:18–21; 51:1–3). The tents will need to be enlarged, and the desolate cities will be inhabited again!

Paul quoted Isaiah 54:1 in Galatians 4:27 and applied the spiritual principle to the church: Even as God blessed Sarah and the Jewish remnant with children, so He would bless the church, though she is only a small company in the world. Paul was not equating Israel with the church or suggesting that the Old Testament promises to the Jews are fulfilled in the church. If we claim the Old Testament Jewish prophecies for the church, then we must claim all of them, the judgments as well as the blessings; and most people do not want to do that!

Israel's restoration to her land will also mean confidence (Isa. 54:4–10). Isaiah gave another one of his "fear not" promises (41:10, 13, 14; 43:1, 5; 44:2, 8; 51:7; 54:14) and explained why there was no need for the nation to be afraid. To begin with, their sins were forgiven (v. 4). Why should they fear the future when God had wiped out the sins of the past (43:25; 44:22)? Yes, the people had sinned greatly against their God, but He forgave them, and this meant a new beginning (40:1–5). They could forget the shame of their sins as a young nation, as recorded in Judges and 1 Samuel, as well as the reproach of their "widowhood" in the Babylonian captivity.

Another reason for confidence is the steadfast love of the Lord (54:5–6). Jehovah is their Maker and would not destroy the people He created for His glory. He is their Redeemer and cannot sell them into the hands of the enemy. He is their Husband and will not break His covenant promises. As an unfaithful wife, Israel had forsaken her Husband, but He had not permanently abandoned her. He only gave her opportunity to see what it was like to live in a land where people worshipped false gods. God would call her back and woo her to Himself (Hos. 2:14–23), and she would no longer be "a wife deserted" (Isa. 54:6 NIV). She felt forsaken (49:14), but God did not give her up.

A third reason for confidence is the dependable promise of God (54:7–10). God had to show His anger at their sin, but now the chastening was over, and they were returning to their land. (On God's anger, see 9:12, 17, and 21.) "With great mercies will I gather thee," He promised. "With everlasting kindness will I have mercy on thee."

Whenever we rebel against God and refuse to listen to His warning, He must chasten us, and He does it in love (Heb. 12:1–11). Our Father cannot permit His children to sin and get away with it. But the purpose of His chastening is to bring us to repentance and enable us to produce "the peaceable fruit of righteousness" (v. 11). When God "spanks" His erring children, He may hurt them, but He never harms them. It is always for our good and His glory.

God kept His promise concerning the flood (Gen. 9:11–17), and He will keep His promises to His people Israel. They can depend on His love, His covenant, and His mercy.

Not only will the captives be set free and the nation restored, but also the city of Jerusalem will be rebuilt (Isa. 54:11–17). If the language here seems extravagant, keep in mind that the prophet saw both an immediate fulfillment and an ultimate fulfillment (Rev. 21:18–21). The remnant rebuilt the temple and the city under the leadership of Zerubbabel the governor, Joshua the high priest, Ezra the scribe, Nehemiah the wall-builder, and the prophets Haggai and Zechariah. But the restored Jerusalem was nothing like what Isaiah described here! For that beautiful city, we must wait till the return of the Lord and the establishing of His kingdom. Then every citizen of Jerusalem will know the Lord (Isa. 54:13), and the city will be free from terror and war (v. 14).

Our Lord quoted the first part of verse 13 in John 6:45. When you read the context, beginning at verse 34, you see that Jesus was speaking about people coming to the Father. "All that the Father gives Me will come to Me" (v. 37 NKJV) does not mean that the Father forces sinners to be saved. People come to Him because they are "taught of God," and the Spirit draws them through the Word. Personal evangelism won't be needed in the New Jerusalem, for all the citizens will know the Lord.

## INVITATION TO THE GENTILES (55:1—56:8)

The Servant died not only for the sins of Israel (53:8), but also for the sins of the whole world (John 1:29; 1 John 4:14). Isaiah makes it clear throughout his book that the Gentiles are included in God's plan. What Isaiah and the other prophets did not know was that believing Jews and Gentiles would one day be united in Jesus Christ in the church (Eph. 3:1–12).

God gives a threefold invitation to the Gentiles: come (Isa. 55:1–5), seek (vv. 6–13), and worship (56:1–8).

**Come (55:1–5).** The invitation is extended to "everyone" and not just to the Jews. Anyone who is thirsting for that which really satisfies (John 4:10–14) is welcome to come. As in Isaiah 25:6, the prophet pictures God's blessings in terms of a great feast, where God is the host.

In the East, water is precious, and an abundance of water is a special blessing (41:17; 44:3). Wine, milk, and bread were staples in their diet. The people were living on substitutes that did not nourish them. They needed "the real thing," which only the Lord could give. In Scripture, both water and wine are pictures of the Holy Spirit (John 7:37–39; Eph. 5:18). Jesus is the "bread of life" (John 6:32–35), and His living Word is like milk (1 Peter 2:2). Our Lord probably had Isaiah 55:2 in mind when He said, "Do not labor for the food which perishes, but for the food which endures to everlasting life" (John 6:27 NKJV).

People have to work hard to dig wells, care for flocks and herds, plant seed, and tend to their vineyards. But the Lord offered to them free everything they were laboring for. If they listen to His Word, they will be inclined to come; for God draws sinners to Himself through the Word (John 5:24). Note the emphasis on hearing in Isaiah 55:2–3.

"The sure mercies of David" involve God's covenant with David (2 Sam. 7) in which He promises that a Descendant would reign on David's throne forever. This, of course, is Jesus Christ (Luke 1:30–33), and the proof that He is God's King is seen in His resurrection from the dead (Acts 13:34–39). Jesus Christ is God's covenant to the Gentiles ("peoples"), and His promises will stand as long as His Son lives, which is forever.

Isaiah 55:5 indicates that God will use Israel to call the Gentiles to salvation, which was certainly true in the early days of the church (Acts 10:1ff.; 13:1ff.) and will be true during the kingdom (Isa. 2:2–4; 45:14; Zech. 8:22). Jerusalem will be the center for worship in the world, and God will be glorified as the nations meet together with Israel to honor the Lord.

**Seek (55:6–13).** When God delivered His people from Babylon and took them safely back to their own land, it was a witness to the other nations. It also gave Israel another opportunity to be a light to the Gentiles (49:6) and bring them to faith in the true and living God. While it was important for Israel to seek the Lord and be wholly devoted to Him, it was also important that they share this invitation with the nations.

What is involved in "seeking the Lord"? For one thing, it means admitting that we are sinners and that we have offended the holy God. It means repenting (55:7), changing one's mind about sin, and turning away from sin and to the Lord. We must turn to God in faith and believe His promise that in mercy He will abundantly pardon. Repentance and faith go together: "repentance toward God, and faith toward our Lord Jesus Christ" (Acts 20:21).

But no one should delay in doing this! The phrase "while he may be found" suggests that, if we do not take His invitation seriously, the invitation may cease while we are delaying. In the parable of the great supper, God closed the door on those who spurned His invitation (Luke 14:16–24; see Prov. 1:20–33). "Behold, now is the accepted time; behold, now is the day of salvation" (2 Cor. 6:2).

It is not a mark of wisdom to try to second-guess God, because His ways and thoughts are far beyond our comprehension (Isa. 55:8–9). We make God after our own image and conclude that He thinks and acts just as we do (Ps. 50:21), and we are wrong! Have you ever tried to explain the grace of God to an unsaved person who thinks that heaven is a "Hall of Fame" for achievers instead of the Father's house for believers? In this world, you work for what you get, and you are suspicious of anything that is free.

How does God go about calling and saving lost sinners? By the power of His Word (Isa. 55:10–11). God's Word is seed (Luke 8:11). Just as the rain and snow are never wasted but accomplish His purposes, so His Word never fails. "The word of our God shall stand forever" (Isa. 40:8). We never know how God will use even a casual word of witness to plant and water the seed in somebody's heart.

Isaiah 55:12–13 describes both the joy of the exiles on their release from captivity and the joy of Israel when they share in that "glorious exodus" in the end of the age and return to their land. When the kingdom is established, all of nature will sing to the Lord (32:13; 35:1–2; 44:23; 52:8–9).

**Worship (56:1–8).** The nation had gone into captivity because she had disobeyed the law of God, particularly the fourth commandment: "Remember the sabbath day, to keep it holy" (Ex. 20:8). This commandment was a special "sign" between God and the Jews (31:12–18; Neh. 9:13–14); it was never given to the Gentiles. The Jews were rebuked for the careless way they treated the Sabbath during their wilderness wanderings (Ezek. 20:10–26) and when they lived in the land (Jer. 17:19–27). Even after their return to the Holy Land after the captivity, the Jews continued to violate the Sabbath (Neh. 13:15–22).

Keep in mind that the Sabbath day is the seventh day of the week, the day that God sanctified when He completed creation (Gen. 2:1–3). Sunday is the Lord's day, the first day of the week, and it commemorates the resurrection of Jesus Christ from the dead. To call Sunday "the Sabbath" or "the Christian Sabbath" is to confuse these two important days. The Sabbath was a sign to the Jews and belongs to the law: You labor for six days, and then you rest. The Lord's day speaks of resurrection and belongs to grace. God's people trust in Christ, and then the works follow.

God never before asked the Gentiles to join the Jews in keeping the Sabbath, but here He does so. He calls the very people He prohibited from entering His covenant nation: foreigners and eunuchs (Deut. 23:1–8). This is another picture of the grace of God (see Acts 8:26ff.). The invitation is still "Everyone come!" It applies to sinners today, but it will apply in a special way when Israel enters her kingdom, the temple services are restored, and the Sabbath is once again a part of Jewish worship.

God's admonition to the remnant to "keep justice, and do righteousness" (Isa. 56:1 NKJV) was not obeyed. When you read Ezra, Nehemiah, Haggai, and Malachi, you discover that the Jews soon forgot God's goodness and returned to their old ways. Taking special time each week to remember the Lord and worship Him helps us to obey His will.

## ACCUSATION AGAINST THE SINNERS (56:9—59:21)

The prophet presented in this section a series of indictments against the disobedient in the nation: the leaders (56:9—57:2), the idolaters (57:3–13), the proud and greedy (vv. 14–21), the hypocritical worshippers (58:1–14), and those responsible for injustice in the land (59:1–21). But even in His wrath, God remembers mercy (Hab. 3:2); for along with these indictments, the Lord pleads with people to humble themselves and submit to Him.

**The leaders of the nation (56:9—57:2).** It was the godless conduct of the leaders that caused Judah to fall to Babylon (Lam. 4:13–14). Had the prophets, priests, and rulers turned to God in repentance and faith, He would have intervened on their behalf, but they persisted in their rebellion. With biting sarcasm, Isaiah called them "blind watchmen" who cannot see the enemy coming, and "sleeping dogs" who could not bark their warning even if they were awake! The leaders were not alert; they loved to sleep, and when they were awake, they loved to eat and drink.

Spiritual leaders are "watchmen" (Ezek. 3:17–21; 33:1–11) who must be awake to the dangers that threaten God's people. They are "shepherds" who must put the care of the flock ahead of their own desires. When the foreign invaders ("beasts of the field") come, the shepherds must protect the flock, no matter what the danger might be. (See Acts 20:18–38 for the description of a faithful spiritual ministry.)

God permitted the unrighteous leaders to live and suffer the terrible consequences of their sins, but the righteous people died before the judgment fell. The godly found rest and peace, and the ungodly went into captivity, and some of them were killed. Rebellious people do not deserve dedicated spiritual leaders. When His people reject His Word and prefer worldly leaders, God may give them exactly what they desire and let them suffer the consequences.

**Idolaters (57:3–13).** During the last days of Judah and Jerusalem, before Babylon came, the land and the city were polluted with idols. King Hezekiah and King Josiah had led the people in destroying the idols and the high places, but as soon as an ungodly king took the throne, the people went right back to their old ways. Both Isaiah and Jeremiah told the people that God would punish them for breaking His law, but they persisted in the ways of the godless nations around them.

God sees idolatry as adultery and prostitution (v. 3). The people knew it was wrong, but they arrogantly practiced their sensual worship ("inflaming yourselves with idols") without shame. You would find them everywhere: visiting the shrine prostitutes under the green trees in the groves, offering their children in the fire in the valley, worshipping under the cliffs and by the smooth boulders, sacrificing up in the mountains, and committing fornication behind the doors of their houses. Publicly and privately, the people were devoted to idols and immorality.

But they were also guilty of consorting with pagan leaders and trusting them for protection instead of trusting God (v. 9). To trust a pagan ruler and his army was the same as trusting the false god that he worshipped (see 30:1–7; 31:1–3). They found false strength in their political alliances and refused to admit that these treaties were hopeless (57:10). God would expose their sin and judge it, and when that happened, their collection of idols ("companies" in v. 13) would not save them.

Anything that we trust other than the Lord becomes our god and therefore is an idol. It may be our training, experience, job, money, friends, or position. One of the best ways to find out whether we have idols in our lives is to ask ourselves, "Where do I instinctively turn when I face a decision or need to solve a problem?" Do we reach for the phone to call a friend? Do we assure ourselves that we can handle the situation ourselves? Or do we turn to God to seek His will and receive His help?

When the storm starts blowing, the idols will blow away like chaff (v. 13). They are "vanity," which means "nothingness." The storm does not make a person; it shows what the person is made of and where his or her faith lies. If we make the Lord our refuge, we have nothing to fear.

**The proud and greedy (57:14–21).** God has a word of encourage-ment for the faithful remnant: The highway will be built and the obstacles removed, so that the exiles might return to the land and serve the Lord. (On the "highway" theme, see 11:16.) God will dwell with them because they are humble in spirit (see 66:2; Ps. 34:18; 51:17). Pride is a sin that God hates (Prov. 6:16–17) and that God resists (1 Peter 5:5–6). God was "enraged" by Israel's "sinful greed" and repeatedly chastened them for it, but they would not change (Isa. 57:17). How often He had "taken them to court" and proved them guilty, yet they would not submit. But now that was over. The time had come for God to heal them, guide them, and comfort them.

**The hypocrites (58:1–14).** God told Isaiah to shout aloud with a voice like a trumpet and announce the sins of the nation. The people went to the temple, obeyed God's laws, fasted, and appeared eager to seek the Lord, but their worship was only an outward show. Their hearts were far from God (1:10–15; 29:13; Matt. 15:8–9). When we worship because it is the popular thing to do, not because it is the right thing to do, then our worship becomes hypocritical.

The Jews were commanded to observe only one fast on the annual Day of Atonement (Lev. 16:29–31), but they were permitted to fast per-sonally if they wished. They complained that nobody seemed to notice what they were doing. Perhaps they were trying to "buy God's blessing" by their fasting. Worshipping God involves more than observing an out-ward ritual; there must be an inward obedience and submission to the Lord (Matt. 6:16–18).

If in my religious duties I am doing what pleases me, and if doing it does not make me a better person, then I am wasting my time, and my worship is only sin. Fasting and fighting do not go together! Yet how many families walk piously out of church at the close of a Sunday worship service, get in the family car, and proceed to argue with each other all the way home!

True fasting will lead to humility before God and ministry to others. We deprive ourselves so that we might share with others and do so to the glory of God. If we fast in order to get something for ourselves from God, instead of to become better people for the sake of others, then we have missed the meaning of worship. It delights the Lord when we delight in the Lord.

**The unjust (59:1–21).** There was a great deal of injustice in the land, with the rich exploiting the poor and the rulers using their authority only to make themselves rich (see 1:17–23; 3:13–15; 5:8–30). The people lifted their hands to worship God, but their hands were stained with blood (1:15, 21). God could not answer their prayers because their sins hid His face from them.

It was a conflict between truth and lies, just as it is today. Isaiah compared the evil rulers to pregnant women giving birth to sin (59:4; Ps. 7:14; Isa. 33:11), to snakes hatching their eggs, and to spiders weaving their webs (Isa. 59:5–6). What they give birth to will only destroy them (James 1:13–15), and their beautiful webs of lies can never protect them.

When people live on lies, they live in a twilight zone and do not know where they are going (Isa. 59:9–11). When trust falls, it creates a "traffic jam," and justice and equity (honesty) cannot make progress (vv. 12–15). God is displeased with injustice, and He wonders that none of His people will intercede or intervene (Prov. 24:11–12). So the Lord Himself intervened and brought the Babylonians to destroy Judah and Jerusalem and to teach His people that they cannot despise His law and get away with it.

God's judgment on His people was a foreshadowing of that final day of the Lord when all the nations will be judged. When it is ended, then "the Redeemer shall come to Zion" (Isa. 59:20), and the glorious kingdom will be established. Israel will be not only God's chosen people but God's cleansed people, and the glory of the Lord will radiate from Mount Zion.

The glory of the Lord in the promised kingdom is the theme of the closing chapters of Isaiah. While we are waiting and praying, "Thy kingdom come," perhaps we should also be interceding and intervening. We are the salt of the earth and the light of the world (Matt. 5:13–16), and God expects us to make a difference.

# QUESTIONS FOR PERSONAL REFLECTION
# OR GROUP DISCUSSION

1. What does Christ's suffering and sacrifice mean to Israel, to the Gentiles, and to rebellious sinners?

2. In Isaiah 54:1–17, what does God promise to restore to His unfaithful wife?

3. What reasons did Israel have to have confidence in God and not be afraid?

4. When believers rebel against God, what is God's response? What is God's motive?

5. What threefold invitation did God give to the Gentiles?

6. What obstacles prevent a person from responding to God's invitation?

7. What is involved in "seeking the Lord"?

8. What was the significance of God's house being called "a house of prayer for all the peoples"?

9. What, in God's view, is true fasting? How can you put this into practice?

# Chapter Thirteen

# THE KINGDOM AND THE GLORY

## (Isaiah 60—66)

"G race is but glory begun," said Jonathan Edwards, "and glory is but grace perfected." Whatever begins with God's grace will lead to God's glory (1 Peter 5:10), and that includes the nation of Israel.

Isaiah began his "Book of Consolation" (chaps. 40—66) by promising that "the glory of the LORD shall be revealed" (40:5). Now he concludes by describing that glory for us. In these seven chapters, he used the word *glory* in one form or another at least twenty-three times. When God's glory is on the scene, everything becomes new.

### THE DAWNING OF A NEW DAY (60:1–22)

"Arise and shine!" is God's "wake-up call" to Jerusalem (v. 1–4), because a new day is dawning for Israel. This light is not from the sun but from the glory of God shining on the city.

God's glory had once dwelt in the tabernacle (Ex. 40:34–38), only to depart because of Israel's sin (1 Sam. 4:21). God's glory then came into the temple (1 Kings 8:11), but it departed when the nation turned to idols (Ezek. 9:3; 10:4, 18; 11:22–23). The glory came to Israel in the person of Jesus Christ (John 1:14), but the nation nailed that glory to a cross.

Today, God's glory dwells in His church (Eph. 2:20–22) and in His people individually (1 Cor. 6:19–20); but one day His glory will be revealed to the earth when He answers His people's prayer: "Thy kingdom come."

The Babylonian captivity had been the nation's darkest hour, but that was not the darkness Isaiah was describing. He was describing the awful darkness that will cover the earth during the day of the Lord (Amos 5:18), when God punishes the nations of the earth for their sins (Isa. 2:12ff.; 13:6ff.). But the prophet was also describing the glorious light that will come to Israel when her Messiah returns to reign in Jerusalem. Then "the earth shall be filled with the knowledge of the glory of the LORD, as the waters cover the sea" (Hab. 2:14). Israel's sons and daughters will come home again (Isa. 60:4, 8–9), and all of them will know the Lord.

It will be the dawning of a new day for the nations of the world as well as for Israel (vv. 3, 10–13). The Gentiles will come to Jerusalem to worship the Lord and to share their wealth (2:2–4; 11:9; 27:13; 56:7; 57:13; 65:25; 66:20). Some people "spiritualize" these promises and apply them to the Gentiles coming to Christ and His church today, but that is not the basic interpretation. Isaiah saw ships and caravans bringing people and wealth to Jerusalem (60:5–7), and the nations that refuse to honor the Lord and His city will be judged (v. 12). Even Israel's old enemies will submit and help to serve the Lord (vv. 10, 14).

In verses 15–22, the Lord describes some of the joys and wonders of the glorious kingdom. The nation will no longer be forsaken but will be enriched by the Gentiles and nursed like a beloved child (vv. 4, 16; 49:23; 61:6). As in the days of King Solomon (1 Kings 10:21, 27), precious metals will be plentiful. It will be a time of peace and safety. "I will make peace your governor and righteousness your ruler" (Isa. 60:17 NIV).

John used some of the characteristics of the millennial Jerusalem when he described the Holy City (Rev. 21—22): The sun never sets; there is no sorrow; the gates never close; etc. But the city Isaiah described is the capital city of the restored Jewish nation, and Jesus Christ shall sit on the throne of David and judge righteously. The Jewish "remnant" will increase and fill the land (Isa. 60:22; 51:2; 54:3).

## THE BEGINNING OF A NEW LIFE (61:1–11)

**The Lord speaks (vv. 1–9).** Jesus quoted from this passage when He spoke in the synagogue in Nazareth, and He applied this Scripture to Himself (Luke 4:16–21). (Note that Isa. 61:1 names the Father, the Son, and the Holy Spirit.) However, He did not quote, "And the day of vengeance of our God" from verse 2 because that day is yet to come (34:8; 35:4; 63:4).

The background of this passage is the "Year of Jubilee" described in Leviticus 25:7ff. Every seven years, the Jews were to observe a "sabbatical year" and allow the land to rest. After seven sabbaticals, or forty-nine years, they were to celebrate the fiftieth year as the "Year of Jubilee." During that year, all debts were canceled, all land was returned to the original owners, the slaves were freed, and everybody was given a fresh new beginning. This was the Lord's way of balancing the economy and keeping the rich from exploiting the poor.

If you have trusted Christ as your Savior, you are living today in a spiritual "Year of Jubilee." You have been set free from bondage; your spiritual debt to the Lord has been paid; you are living in "the acceptable year of the Lord." Instead of the ashes of mourning, you have a crown on your head, for He has made you a king (Rev. 1:6). You have been anointed with the oil of the Holy Spirit, and you wear a garment of righteousness (Isa. 61:3, 10).

In her days of rebellion, Israel was like a fading oak and a waterless garden (1:30), but in the kingdom, she will be like a watered garden (58:11) and a tree (oak) of righteousness (61:3). But all of God's people should be His trees (Ps. 1:1–3), "the planting of the LORD, that he might be glorified" (Isa. 61:3).

In their kingdom Year of Jubilee, the Jewish people will rebuild, repair, and restore their land, and the Gentiles will shepherd Israel's flocks and herds and tend to their crops. Instead of being farmers and shepherds, the Jews will

184 \ Be Comforted

be priests and ministers! God will acknowledge them as His firstborn (Ex. 4:22) and give them a double portion of His blessing (Isa. 61:7; Deut. 21:17).

The "everlasting covenant" of Isaiah 61:8 is described in Jeremiah 31:31–37 and includes the blessings of the new covenant that Jesus Christ instituted by His death (Heb. 10:1–18; Matt. 26:28). Note that Isaiah 61:9 speaks of the Jews' "descendants." Those who enter into the millennial kingdom will marry, have families, and enjoy God's blessings on the earth for a thousand years (Rev. 20:1–5). They will study God's Word from generation to generation (Isa. 59:21).

**The prophet speaks (vv. 10–11).** Isaiah is speaking on behalf of the remnant who are praising God for all He has done. They rejoice that He has cleansed them and clothed them and turned their desert into a fruitful garden (55:10). They have gone from a funeral to a wedding!

## THE BESTOWING OF A NEW NAME (62:1–12)

**God will not hold His peace (vv. 1–5).** The "I" in verse 6 indicates that the Lord is the speaker. God promises to keep speaking and working till His purposes for Jerusalem are fulfilled. This is not only for the sake of Zion but also for the sake of the nations of the world. There will be no righteousness and peace on this earth till Jerusalem gets her new name and becomes a crown of glory to the Lord.

As an unfaithful wife, Israel was "forsaken" by the Lord, but not "divorced" (50:1–3). Her trials will all be forgotten when she receives the new name, "Hephzibah," which means "my delight is in her." God delights in His people and enjoys giving them His best. The old name "Desolate" will be replaced by "Beulah," which means "married" (see also 54:1). When a bride marries, she receives a new name. In the case of Israel, she is already married to Jehovah, but she will get a new name when she is reconciled to Him.

**The watchmen must not hold their peace (vv. 6–12).** God gave His people leaders to guide them, but they were not faithful (56:10). Now He gives them faithful watchmen, who constantly remind God of His promises. "Give him no rest till he establishes Jerusalem and makes her the praise of the earth" (62:7 NIV). What an encouragement to us to "pray for the peace of Jerusalem" (Ps. 122:6).

God promises that the Jews will never again lose their harvests to the enemy but will enjoy the fruit of their labors in the very courts of His sanctuary. What a privilege! According to Ezekiel 40—48, there will be a millennial temple, and the Jews will worship the Lord there. Having received their Messiah, they will now clearly understand the spiritual meaning of their worship. Today, their minds are veiled (2 Cor. 3:14–18), but then, their eyes will be opened.

Isaiah 62:10 is another reference to the "highway" (11:16; 40:3–5), and there is an urgency about these words. The Lord is about to arrive, and the people must get the road ready! When the work is completed, they must lift a banner to signal they are ready.

"See, your Savior comes!" (62:11 NIV). This is a proclamation that goes to the ends of the earth! And when He comes, He shares more new names: Israel is called "the Holy People" and "the Redeemed of the LORD," and Jerusalem is called "Sought After, the City No Longer Deserted" (v. 12 NIV).

God will have no rest till He accomplishes His purposes for His people, and the world will have no peace till He succeeds. He asks us to "give him no rest" (v. 7) but to intercede for Israel and Jerusalem, for the prayers of His people are an important part of the program of God.

## THE ANNOUNCING OF A NEW VICTORY (63:1—64:12)

The prophet looks ahead in 63:1–6 and sees Jesus Christ returning from the Battle of Armageddon that climaxes the day of the Lord (Rev. 19:11–21). Edom is named here as a representative of the nations that have oppressed the Jews. Bozrah was one of its main cities, and its name means "grape gathering." This is significant since the image here is that of the winepress

186 \ Be Comforted

(Joel 3:13; Rev. 14:17–20). The name "Edom" means "red" and was a nickname for Esau (Gen. 25:30).

The ancient winepress was a large, hollowed rock into which the grapes were put for the people to tread on them. The juice ran out a hole in the rock and was caught in vessels. As the people crushed the grapes, some of the juice would splash on their garments. Our Lord's garments were dyed with blood as the result of the great victory over His enemies (Rev. 19:13).

When Jesus came to earth the first time, it was to inaugurate "the acceptable year of the LORD" (Isa. 61:2; Luke 4:19). When He comes the second time, it will be to climax "the day of vengeance of our God" (Isa. 63:4; 61:2). The enemy will be crushed like grapes and forced to drink their own blood from the cup of God's wrath (51:17; Jer. 25:15–16). These images may not appeal to sophisticated people today, but the Jews in that day fully understood them.

Then the prophet looked back at what God has done for Israel (Isa. 63:7–14). He praised God for His lovingkindness and goodness, for the pity and love bestowed on Israel. God identified with their sufferings (v. 9; Judg. 10:16; Deut. 32:10–12) as He does with His people today (1 Peter 5:7). The Jews asked, "Where is our God who did wonders for His people? Why is He not working on our behalf?"

The prophet looked up and called on God to bare His arm and display His power (Isa. 63:15—64:12). For Abraham's sake, for Israel's sake, because God is their Father, he pled for a demonstration of power just as God did in the ancient days.

He asked God to "look down" (63:15) and to "come down" (64:1). This is one of the greatest "revival prayers" found in Scripture. Just as God came down in fire at Sinai (Ex. 19:16–19), so let Him come down again and reveal His awesome power to the nations. They trust in dead idols, so let them see what the living God of Israel can do!

Why is God not working wonders? They have sinned (Isa. 64:5–6) and must confess their sins and turn from them. If our righteousness is filthy, what must our sins look like in His sight! According to verse 4, God has planned for His people wonderful things beyond their imagination, but their sins prevent Him from sharing His blessings (see 1 Cor. 2:9; Eph. 3:20–21). Is there any hope? Yes, because God is a forgiving Father and a patient Potter (Jer. 18). He can cleanse us and make us anew if we will let Him have His way.

This prayer (and the believing remnant) ends with a question: Why is God silent? His temple has been destroyed, His glorious land has been ravaged, and His people are in exile. "After all this, O LORD, will you hold yourself back? Will you keep silent and punish us beyond measure?" (Isa. 64:12 NIV). God's reply is found in the next two chapters.

## THE BLESSING OF A NEW CREATION (65:1–25)

"I will not keep silence, but will recompense, even recompense into their bosom" (65:6). God now replies.

First, He announces that His salvation will go to the Gentiles (v. 1), even though they did not seek the Lord or experience the blessings that He gave to Israel. Paul applied this verse to the Gentiles in Romans 10:19–20. If Israel did not want what God had to offer, then He would give it to others. (See Luke 14:16–24; 21:10; Acts 28:23–31 for other illustrations of this divine principle.)

Then, God describes the sins of His people that kept Him from answering their prayers (Isa. 65:2–7). They resisted His grace and His loving appeals, though He held out His arms to them and spoke to them through His Word (Rom. 10:21). They went their own way (Isa. 53:6) and provoked Him with their evil worship of false gods, getting involved with the occult and demons. They ate food that was unclean and openly worshipped idols in the high places. And yet these rebellious people considered themselves to be better than others! "I am holier than thou!"

God then explains that He had to judge the nation for her sins (65:8–16). He called the Babylonians to be His instrument of punishment to teach His people that they could not sin and get away with it. However, in mercy He preserved a remnant—like a few grapes rescued from the winepress—and that remnant would return to the land and restore the nation. When His people sincerely seek Him (v. 10), then He will bless them (2 Chron. 7:14).

"The Valley of Achor" was the place where Achan was stoned to death because he disobeyed the Lord (Josh. 7). When the Lord restores His estranged wife, Israel, the Valley of Achor will become for them "a door of hope" (Hos. 2:15).

In Isaiah 65:11–16, God sees two kinds of people in the land: those who forsake the Lord and those who serve the Lord. ("My Servant" has now become "My servants.") Those who forsake the Lord ignore His temple and worship false gods, such as fortune and destiny (in v. 11, "that troop" and "that number"). These disobedient Jews will not live but be destroyed, and those who do survive will not enjoy it. In fact, their very names will be used as curses in the years to come!

God saves the best for the last: His description of "the new heavens and new earth" (the millennial kingdom) in 65:17—66:24.

This is not the same as John's "new heaven and new earth" (Rev. 21:1ff.), because the characteristics Isaiah gives do not fit the eternal state. As far as we know, in the eternal state people will not get old or die (Isa. 65:20), nor will there be any danger of losing anything to invaders (vv. 21–23).

Jerusalem will be a source of joy, not only to the Lord but to the whole earth. It will be a city of holiness, harmony, and happiness. During the millennial kingdom, people will work, and God will bless their labors. People will pray, and God will answer (v. 24). Nature will be at peace (v. 25) because the curse will be lifted.

## THE BIRTH OF THE NEW NATION (66:1–24)

Of course, the remarkable thing will be the "birth of a nation" as Israel takes center stage on the international scene (vv. 7–9). The return of the Jews to their land will be as swift as the birth of a baby. Israel's "travail" will be "the day of the Lord" or "the time of Jacob's trouble" (Jer. 30:7), when God will purify His people and prepare them for the coming of their Messiah. Political Israel was born on May 14, 1948, but "the new Israel" will be "born in a day" when they believe on Jesus Christ. Jerusalem will experience joy, peace, and satisfaction (Isa. 66:10–14). Like a nursing baby, she will find health and peace in the arms of the Lord. "Peace like a river" reminds us of Isaiah's words to Ahaz (85:5–8) and God's promises in 41:18 and 48:18.

There will be a new temple (66:1–6; Ezek. 40—48), but the ceremonies of worship can never take the place of a humble heart. God does not live in buildings; He dwells with those who submit to Him. Stephen quoted Isaiah 66:1–2 in his defense before the Jews (Acts 7:48–50), and Paul referred to these words in his address to the Athenian philosophers (17:24).

In Isaiah's day, were God's people trembling at His Word? No, they were not. Instead, they were going through the motions of worship without having a heart for God. The people were not sacrificing the animals; they were murdering them! Because their hearts were far from God (Isa. 29:13), their offerings were as unclean things to the Lord. It is the heart of the worshipper that determines the value of the offering.

God's hand will bring blessing to His servants but "indignation toward His enemies" (66:14), and Isaiah described that "indignation" in verses 15–18. The day of the Lord will be a storm of judgment with fire and whirlwinds and with the sword of God, "And those slain by the Lord shall be many."

Who will be slain? Those who have disobeyed God's law in their eating and their worshipping (vv. 17–18). Instead of worshipping the true and living God, they turned to pagan idols and pagan practices. It is not enough to be "religious"; we must serve Him according to what He says in His Word (8:20).

The book closes with a description of messengers going to the ends of the earth to announce what God has done for Israel (66:19). The result will be a flow of people to Jerusalem (see 50:3–14; 66:12) to bring offerings to the

Lord. In the past, Gentile nations came to Jerusalem to attack and destroy, but in the Kingdom Age, they will come to worship and glorify God.

The book ends on a seemingly negative note describing worshippers looking at the desecrated and decayed corpses of the rebels (v. 24). The Valley of Hinnom (Hebrew *ge hinnom* = *Gehenna* in the Greek) is a picture of judgment (30:33). Jesus used it to picture hell (Mark 9:43–48). The people who come to Jerusalem to worship will also go outside the city to this "garbage dump" and be reminded that God is a consuming fire (Jer. 7:32).

Throughout his book, Isaiah has presented us with alternatives: Trust the Lord and live, or rebel against the Lord and die. He has explained the grace and mercy of God and offered His forgiveness. He has also explained the holiness and wrath of God and warned of His judgment. He has promised glory for those who will believe and judgment for those who scoff. He has explained the foolishness of trusting man's wisdom and the world's resources.

The prophet calls the professing people of God back to spiritual reality. He warns against hypocrisy and empty worship. He pleads for faith, obedience, a heart that delights in God, and a life that glorifies God.

"'There is no peace,' saith the LORD, 'unto the wicked'" (Isa. 48:22; 57:21); for in order to have peace, you must have righteousness (32:17). The only way to have righteousness is through faith in Jesus Christ (Rom. 3:19–31).

Isaiah's message has been "Be comforted by the Lord!" (see Isa. 12:1; 40:1–2; 49:13; 51:3, 19; 52:9; 54:11; 57:18; 61:2; 66:13). But God cannot comfort rebels! If we are sinning against God and comfortable about it, something is radically wrong. That false comfort will lead to false confidence, and that will lead to the chastening hand of God.

"Seek ye the LORD while he may be found" (55:6).

"Though your sins be as scarlet, they shall be as white as snow" (1:18).

"O LORD, I will praise You; though You were angry with me, Your anger is turned away, and You comfort me" (12:1 NKJV).

*Be comforted!*

# QUESTIONS FOR PERSONAL REFLECTION
## OR GROUP DISCUSSION

1. What evidence have you seen that God finishes what He begins? What unfinished areas do you look forward to Him completing?

2. What process often lies between grace and glory according to 1 Peter 5:10?

3. What becomes "new" when a person trusts Christ as Savior and Lord (see 2 Cor. 5:17)?

4. What victory does Isaiah look ahead to in 63:1–6? What great blessing on Israel did the prophet look back on in Isaiah 63:7–14?

5. How does God describe His attitude toward His people and their response to Him (see Isa. 65:1–7)?

6. Who was, and will be, saved in the remnant?

7. What do you look forward to in the new heaven and new earth?

8. What are the qualities of a person about whom God says, "But to this one I look" (Isa. 66:2)?

9. What does Isaiah call people to do? Warn them against? Plead for?

10. Who will be comforted? How? Why them?